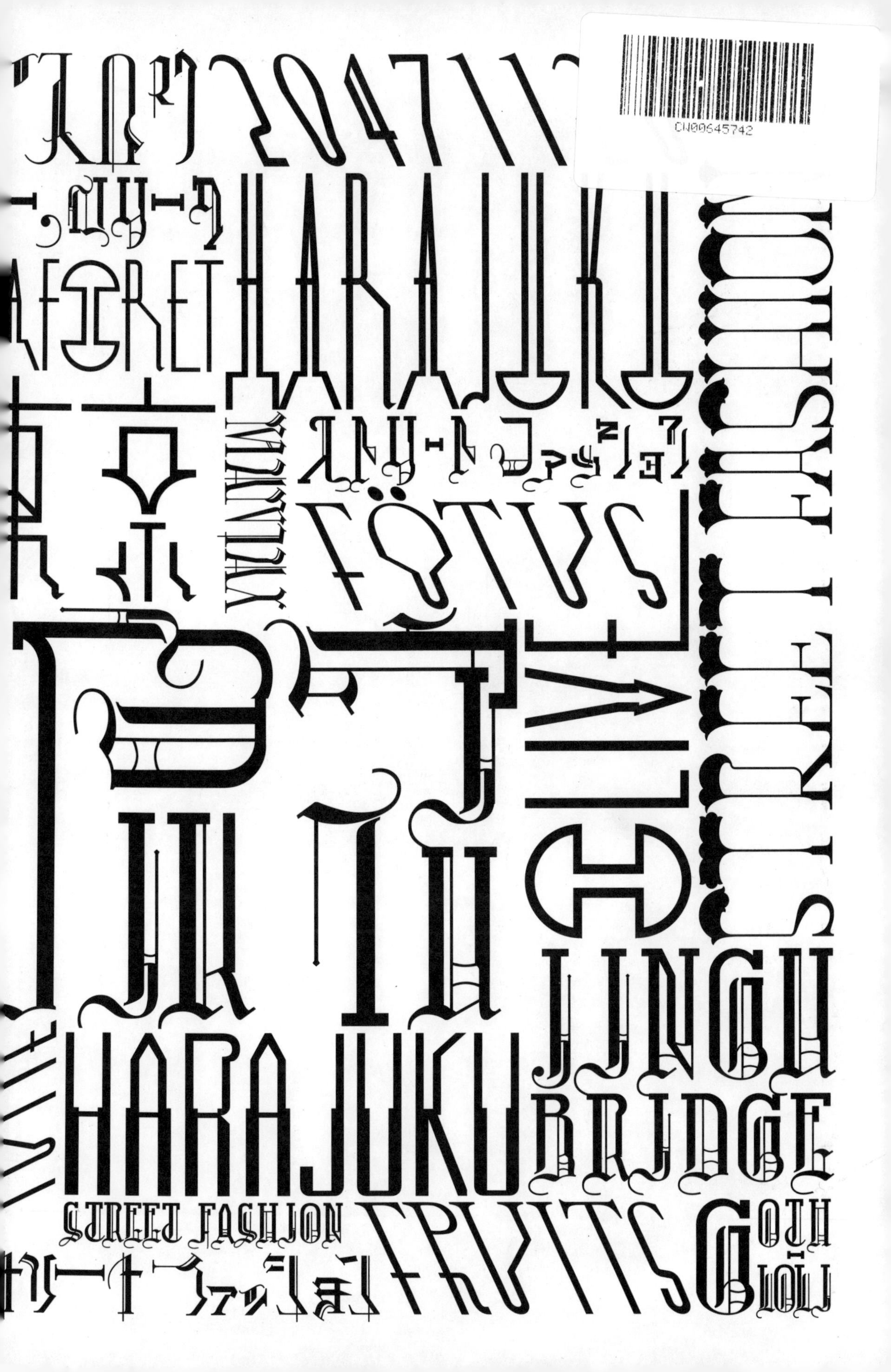
HARAJUKU
HARAJUKU
JINGU
BRIDGE
STREET FASHION
FRUITS
GOTH LOLI

TOKYO STREET STYLE

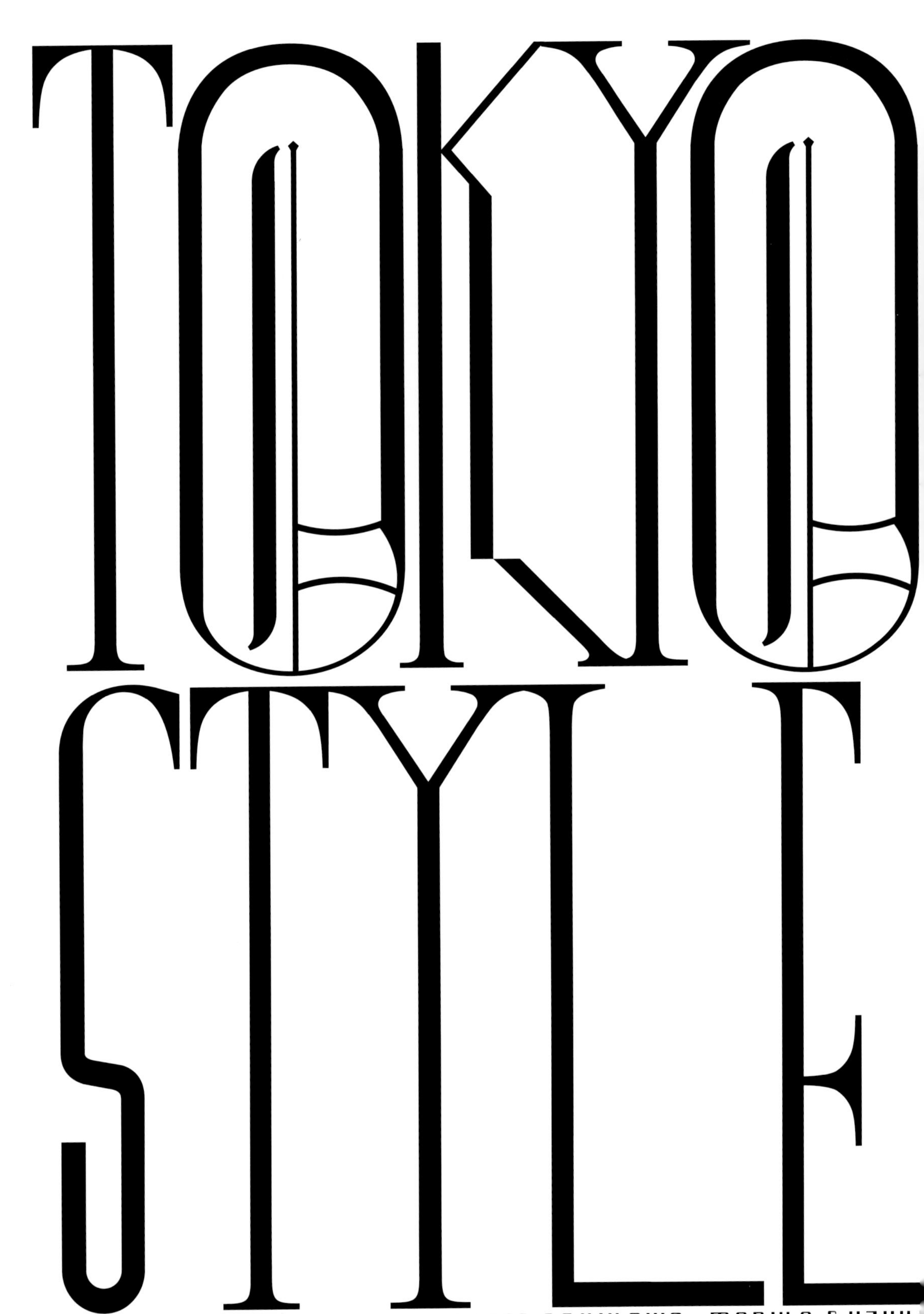

Essays by TAKEJI HIRAKAWA MAKOTO SEKIKAWA MARIKO SUZUK

STREET FASHION IN HARAJUKU

Edited by IVAN VARTANIAN BY TIFFANY GODOY
KEIKO HIRAYAMA TETSUYA SUZUKI

Thames & Hudson

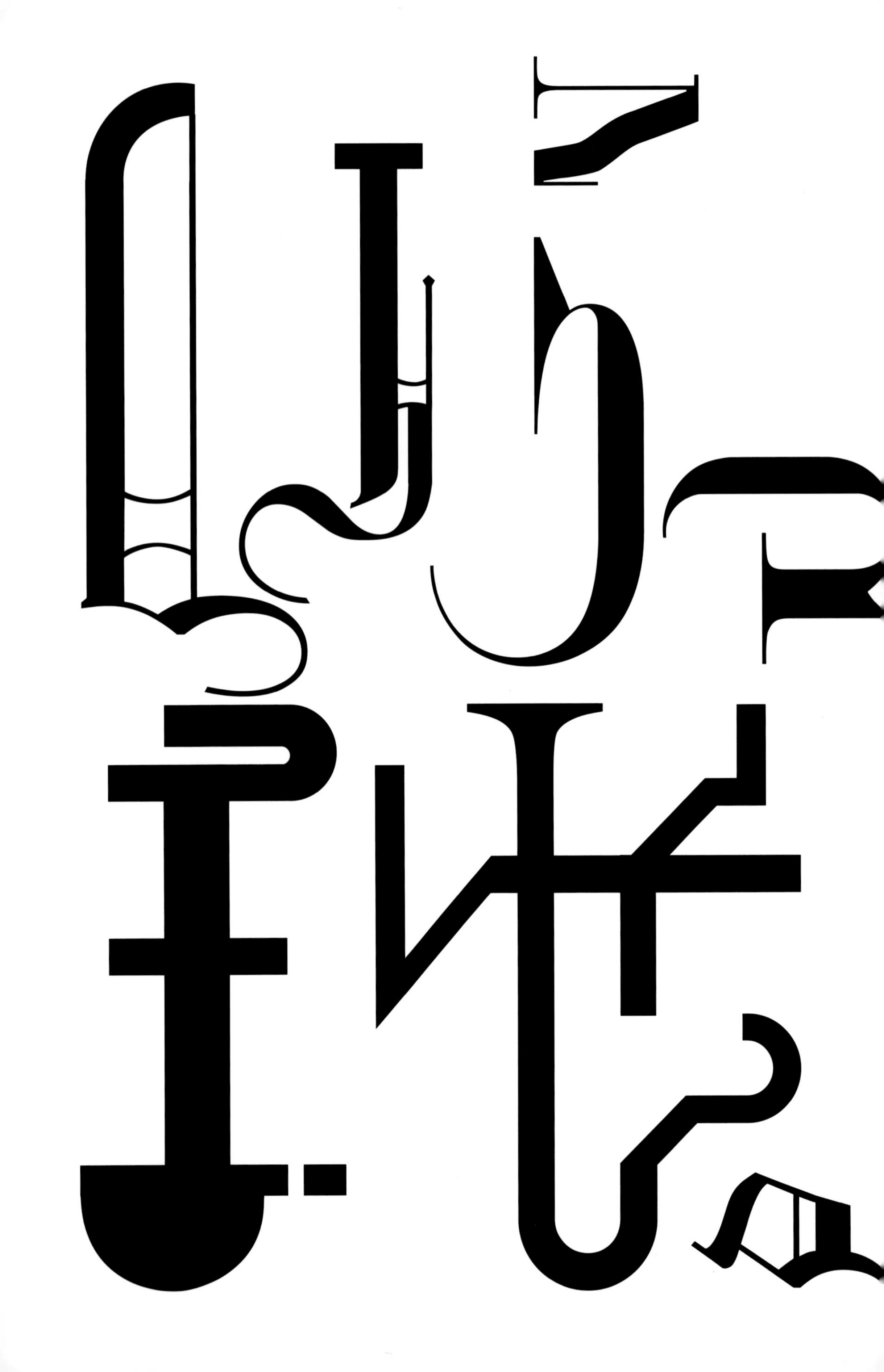

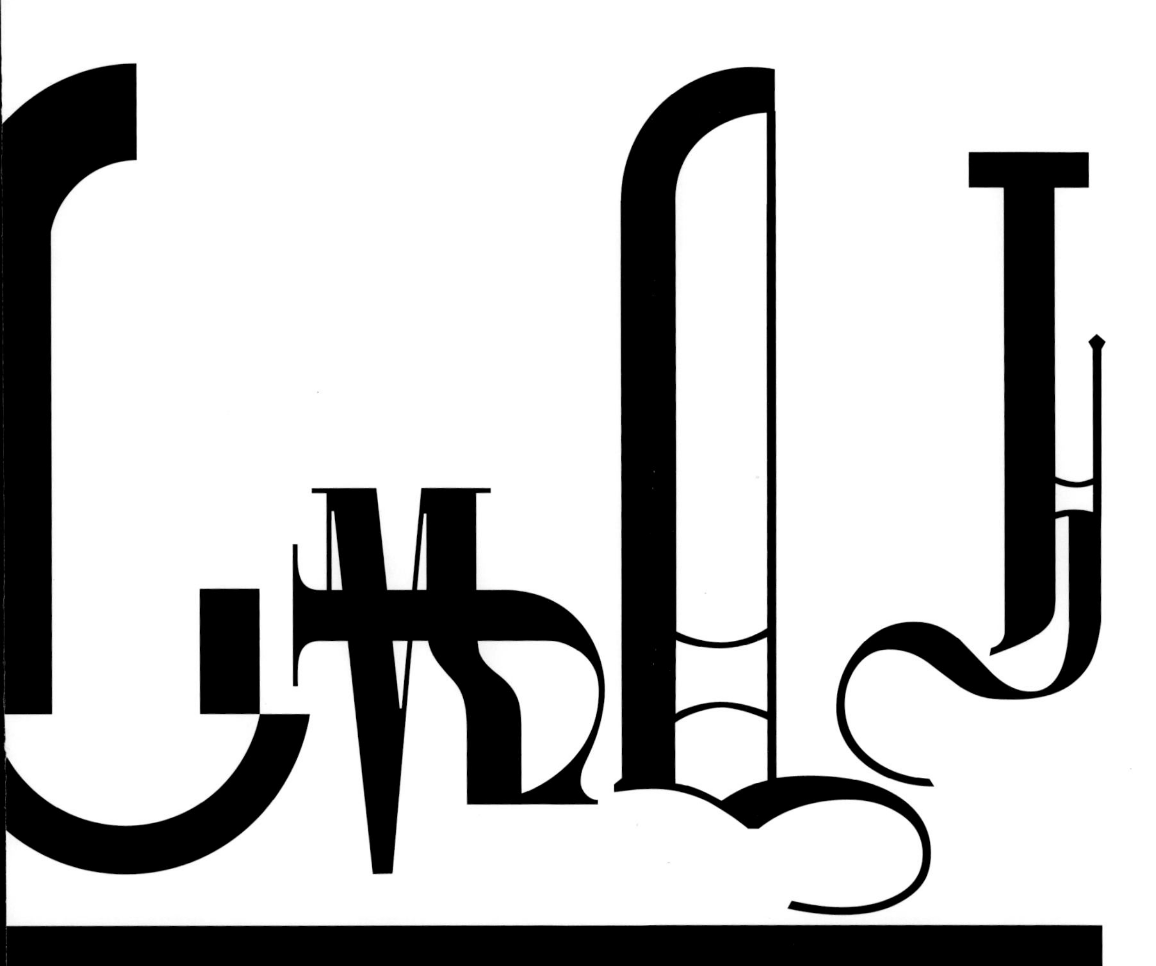

Tokyo Street Style was produced by
Ivan Vartanian / Goliga Books, Inc.
www.goliga.com

Art Direction by
Tomoyuki Yonezu (Erotyka)

Layout by
Mariko Kobori
Yasuhiro Takeuchi (VENUE)
Miyuki Hentona

Production and
co-edition coordination by
Rico Komanoya (ricorico)

Additional research and
editorial assistance by
Maki Minegishi, Yumiko Yata, and Kyoko Wada

First published in the United Kingdom in 2008 by
Thames & Hudson Ltd, 181A High Holborn,
London WC1V 7QX

www.thamesandhudson.com

British Library Cataloguing-in-Publication Data
A catalogue record for this book is available from the British Library

ISBN: 978-0-500-51403-0

Printed and bound in China

THE ROOTS

KAWAII

CYBER & BEYOND

Goth-Loli

Ura-Hara

Post

HARAJUKU MADE ME DO IT

BY TIFFANY GODOY AND IVAN VARTANIAN

The Harajuku scene has put Tokyo on the world's fashion map—alongside London, Paris, New York, and Milan. Any designer worth their pin cushion and collection of *Visionaire* has to pay attention to what's happening in "Tokyo" (shorthand reference for what's happening in Harajuku). Harajuku, a one-square-mile haven within the city, has become the epicenter of current style. Waiting for the light to change at the main intersection—the corner of Omotesando and Meiji-dori—offers a mesmerizing panoply of silhouettes, colors, textures, and labels; the aggressively stylized, the excessively accessorized, the unapologetically restless inventing (or buying) the future in this melting pot of fashion, youth, and shopping. You walk into Harajuku and—*bam!*—you are in outer space. Since the emergence of the Harajuku scene, numerous magazines have reported on and helped steer its trends, but their impact is minor compared to the influence of the action on the streets themselves. So immediate and rapid is the turnover of trends, and so attenuated the attention of the fashion-forward, that subtle differences make dramatic statements.

While the Harajuku district has long been a spot for a domestic audience to come into contact with foreign culture and style, today the influence has reversed: foreign fashion leaders are taking notice and being influenced by what's happening on Harajuku's streets. Japan's top designers are now being invited to collaborate with the Western vanguard: Fendi collaborates with Nigo, Prada parties with Hiroshi Fujiwara as DJ.

One Western source that continued to influence Harajuku fashion (well, at least it was a source of inspiration) was *i-D* magazine—*i-D* presented a mélange of club culture, bands, DJs, and the reaction of the people on the street to these movements and sounds and the people that created them. This format became a model for the influential Japanese fashion and culture magazine *CUTiE*. Couture and high fashion had previously been considered solely the province of Europe and America, so for Japanese designers, the prospect of showing a collection in Paris was equivalent to playing in the major league. With the advent of the Harajuku scene, this was no longer the case. Suddenly the established fashion world was on the outside looking in, and the Western fashion establishment now wants to work with the Harajuku avant-garde. Nike's CEO Mark Parker has been collaborating with designer Hiroshi Fujiwara. Marc Jacobs works with art impresario Takashi Murakami. Pop star Gwen Stefani professes her love for the Harajuku girl and copies her style onstage. Prada has moved into Tokyo and erected a tower-like shop designed by renowned architects Herzog & De Meuron. And the hyper-store Omotesando has been converted into a veritable gallery of luxury brand flagship stores.

* * *

Cross-cultural ferment of this sort began at the end of World War II, when Harajuku was the site of U.S. military residences and shops catering to the servicemen's families. Japanese youths flocked to the area to see Western products and be exposed to Western culture. By the 1960s the neighborhood had become an established meeting ground for Japanese youths, fostering commercial development in the area.

The 1960s and 1970s saw the emergence of youth culture both in the West—marked by the social revolution and unrest highlighted by the events of Paris 1968, Woodstock, and the Vietnam war—and in Japan, where a new generation saw its country rise from postwar ashes to become the second most powerful economy in the world by the 1980s. From these newly arisen and empowered youth were born the creators of the Harajuku scene.

The first wave of young creators to occupy the neighborhood in the 1960s and 1970s were drawn to its potential as a market for new fashion because of the kids who gathered there, kids with a desire to forge something new. This first generation of designers worked from scratch, creating a brand-new business model. Soon these small efforts grew into major apparel companies now known as "DC" (Designer Character) brands. Such fashion forces as Yohji Yamamoto and Comme des Garçons began as DC brands.

Built in Harajuku in 1978, the Laforet shopping center quickly became the core of the youth scene and the locus for new fashion businesses. As Japan entered its economic boom years during the 1980s, people started spending lavishly on consumer goods. This healthy and robust consumer economy was crucial to the development of the next generation of designers and brands, who seemed to have a preternatural understanding of trade, trends, and marketing. The Harajuku creators of the 1980s and 1990s, like their predecessors from the previous decade, continued the tradition of inventing new business paradigms alongside their similarly new designs. Though Japanese culture holds a strong allegiance to tradition, Harajuku is the antithesis. Harajuku has been known as a locus of youthful energy—chasing after the newest thing—since its inception as a design district. It is perhaps for this reason that Harajuku, as an idea as much as a place, is inextricably linked with youth culture.

When the hyperbolic growth of Japan's economy ended with a crash in the early 1990s, the reverberations shook many of the core values and beliefs (which included an expectation that Japan would see unlimited economic expansion) that had become fundamental to Japanese identity. Big business no longer dominated the market, but was seen as just as risky as small business, thus creating a level playing field for all new ventures and encouraging a new sense of possibility among start-ups. Suddenly, anyone could be a contender. This burgeoning sense of opportunity coincided with a reaction in several underground scenes that a creeping homogenization of Harajuku street fashion had occurred during the boom years, turning the first phase of development of Japan's street fashion into something easily assimilated and replicated in the broader popular culture and robbing it of its edge.

The neighborhood's compactness and specificity of place have permitted not just trends but microtrends to flourish and then subside with such speed that fashion seems to change from moment to moment. The designers, stylists, and fashion editors interviewed for this book were wary—even shocked—at the idea of trying to track and define styles that evolve and splinter at such a rapid pace. For all the emphasis in Japanese culture on maintaining a connection to the past, there is an equivalent push toward constant change, to find the new and the next. The street nature of Harajuku styles, and the way in which design develops here—more to do with editing and remixing than with setting down new tracks—also contribute to the ephemerality of Harajuku street style. Each look is an amalgam of many other styles, strategies, incidents, and whims.

Though Harajuku's fashion history dates back fifty years, this book focuses mostly on the styles that have emerged from the post-bubble era of the early 1990s to today. Within this relatively brief period, multiple distinct styles have evolved: *Kawaii,* Cyber-Punk, Goth-Loli, Ura-Hara, Fushigi-chan ("mystery kid," for kids whose fashion garble is totally inscrutable), as well as derivatives of each. Across them all, there are certain commonalities that hint at some of the core methods used in Harajuku fashion. Everything is selected with extreme care and a heightened attention to detail. It's not enough to wear a bracelet, it has to be coordinated with all the other elements of a look (makeup, hair, shoes) as well as with the wearer's friends' or partner's look for the day. It also has to either coordinate with the seasons or purposefully not do so. Just who determines the details of these different styles is explored in this book through profiles of many of the pivotal creators and influencers—characters with such charisma and notoriety that they can start a trend with a mere nod of the head, approving some unexpected design twist or snip of a garment.

Another key to understanding Harajuku street culture lies in Japan's relationship with the outside world. In many, and perhaps most, instances there is a total disconnect between what something is and what it's *supposed* to mean. Punk can be cute. Micro-mini skirts aren't sexy. Ghoulish makeup isn't macabre. Hip-hop is a state of mind rather than a reference to a specific cultural experience. The extremes to which average youth use body piercing as personal adornment have nothing to do with tribal beats, sexuality, or counter-culturalism. Here, it is pure fashion.

* * *

What has developed in Harajuku has radically altered what had been fashion's normal business practices and marketing strategies. Traditional couture is preoccupied with structure, superlative craftsmanship, and exquisite materials, used in ways that create new forms: a type of wearable architecture. Street fashion, on the other hand, is entirely about pop culture. T-shirts, denim, and off-the-rack clothes are staples of this wardrobe. Until relatively recently, there was a clear distinction between couture, prêt-à-porter, sportswear, and street fashion. While there is evidence of an increasing cross-pollination in all sectors, the extent of intermingling in Harajuku is remarkable. Here are limited-edition shoes and T-shirts, tailor-made sweatshirts, and embroidered casual wear, which, given their limited numbers, are essentially word-of-mouth sales.

Many of the creators featured in this book are under forty years of age, and have built successful fashion brands in a relatively short amount of time. Entrepreneurial, media-savvy, creative, and determined, they represent a young, vital energy in Japanese society that harks back to the earlier achievements of the postwar generation.

Japan's youth culture has always evolved in relationship to what preceded it, with the kids—typical of youth everywhere—seeking a new identity separate from the one dictated by standard social norms. What characterizes Harajuku's street fashion is precisely this search, which is clearly expressed in the costumes these kids wear. Harajuku street fashions are both a form of self-expression and a way to advertise a specific community identity—mostly informed through shared stylistic qualities.

All the developments of the recent Harajuku scene—street fashion, guerrilla marketing, and limited editions, along with the explosion of individual designers and customizers—created an environment in which Japanese kids have been able to co-opt foreign styles, creating something particular to Japan: a kind of fashion nationalism. Since the postwar economic boom years, Japan has become a country committed to shopping. Despite the downturn of the 1990s, shopping has remained an integral part of the national character, and a particularly powerful way to assert identity among the youth. The development of youth culture as an economic force internationally has accelerated the rate of trend turnover in Japan, which occurs at an astounding speed.

In Harajuku, clothing is a reaction to the immediate reality of the street. Influences can appear right before you, just walking down Omotesando. There is a strange sort of democratic idolatry found there. Celebrities are not the only fashion icons, but all those tangentially involved in the business—designers, stylists, shop staff, hair stylists, and even publicists—enjoy a great deal of notoriety within the scene (well, at least the successful ones do). Even the kids who buy the latest trends can have their moment in the sun. Teams of photographers from street-snap magazines like *FRUiTS* and *TUNE* are regularly stationed along Harajuku's main drag, capturing the kids and turning them, at least for an issue, into fashion celebrities and innovators. Where else can you walk down the street expecting to be scouted by camera crews?

In the scene's frenetic jump from style to style to style, there is a consistent lack of complacence—a style deficit disorder driving the relentless hunt for the new. Trends appear in a flash and disappear just as quickly. Kids move in and out of styles with amazing agility. One-time stars of the scenes are washed-up has-beens weeks later. Anyone who stays put is left behind: fashion plate leftovers. More roadkill on fashion's street runway. Harajuku is a headless beast that is at the mercy of its desires and restlessness. Welcome to Harajuku. *Irasshaimase!*

www.styledeficitdisorder.com

THE LAY OF THE LAND

HARAJUKU STATION

Harajuku and Shibuya stations are neighboring stops on the Yamanote line, which runs in a loop around the center of Tokyo. Though separated by a mere two-minute train ride (or a ten-minute walk along Meiji-dori), the fashion trends and styles associated with these two stations are distinct. Harajuku station abuts the precinct of Meiji Jingu, part of the Yoyogi Park complex, which is owned by the imperial family. The path from Harajuku station to the Meiji Jingu shrine inside the park is a broad, gravel-lined walkway that winds through a thick forest—a marked contrast to the crowded cinderblock alleys extending from the east side of the station that are part of Harajuku's shopping core.

MEIJI JINGU

At the south exit of Harajuku station, the Jingu-bashi bridge leads to the large main gate of the shrine Meiji Jingu. Built to traverse the train lines underneath and adjoin the intersection that connects Omotesando with Yoyogi, the bridge is only 130-feet long. With arches lining one side and large poured-cement lanterns at either end, the bridge is like the proscenium of a theatrical stage. The raised footbridges that straddle the avenues nearby give pedestrians an elevated view of the bridge. So it is natural that it functions like a theater, in this case of fashion, mostly of the Goth-Loli ilk. Jingu-bashi gained notoriety in the late 1990s when visual-kei bands and their groupies gathered there for ad hoc performances.

Takeshita - dori

This densely crowded pedestrian shopping street begins at the east exit of Harajuku station and runs about one quarter mile. Once the neighborhood's local shopping street purveying groceries and rice, it began its transformation into a fashion avenue when young creators moved in during the early 1970s in search of affordable rent. On weekends Takeshita-dori is sensory overload, packed with out-of-town visitors, a countless number of clothing shops, Puri-kura (print club) photo-sticker shops, and dessert-crepe vendors.

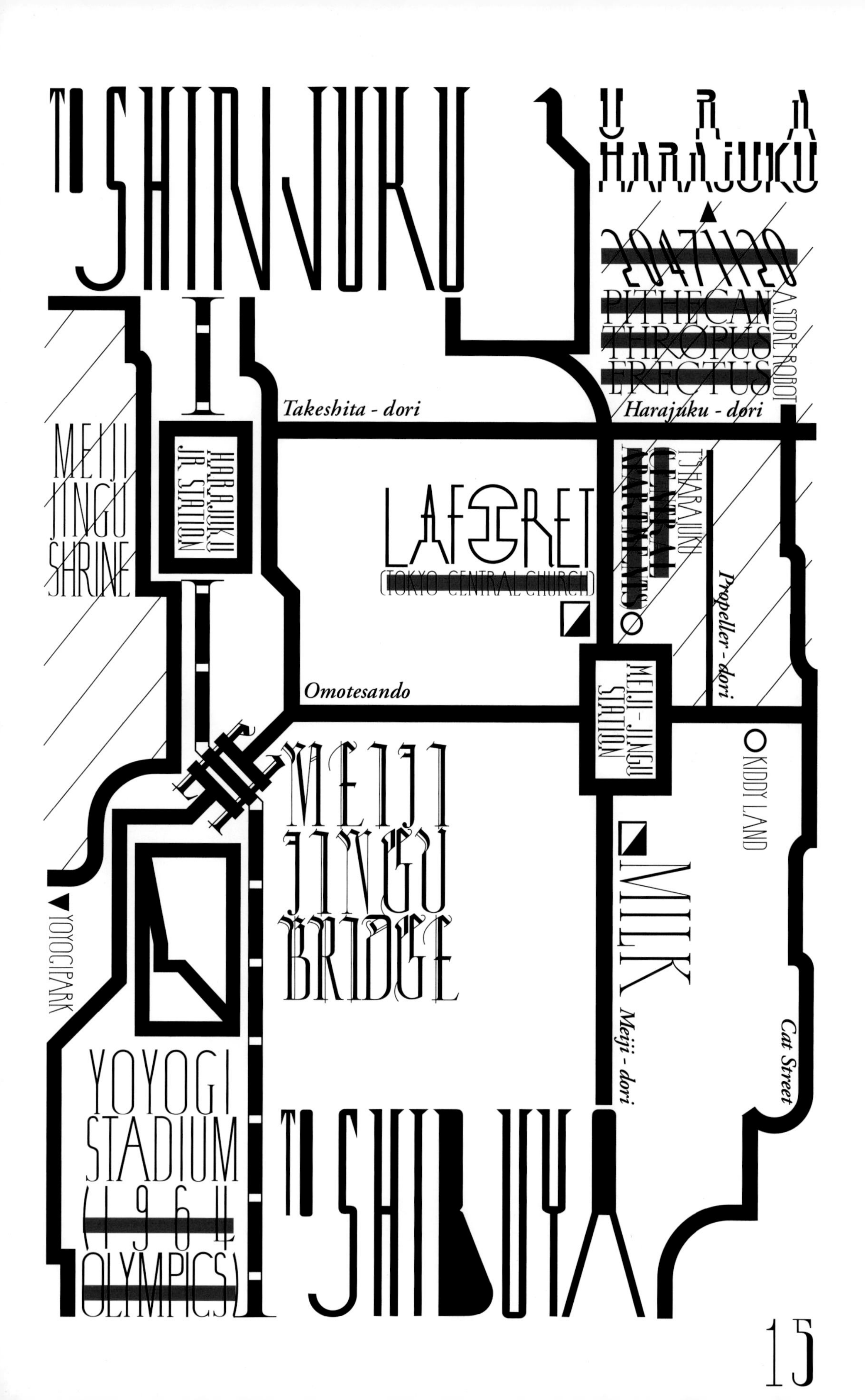
SHINJUKU
URA HARAJUKU
PITHECANTHROPUS ERECTUS
A STORE ROBOT
Takeshita - dori
Harajuku - dori
MEIJI JINGU SHRINE
HARAJUKU JR STATION
LAFORET
(TOKYO CENTRAL CHURCH)
CENTRAL APARTMENTS
T'S HARAJUKU
Propeller - dori
Omotesando
MEIJI-JINGU STATION
KIDDY LAND
MEIJI JINGU BRIDGE
MILK
YOYOGI PARK
Meiji - dori
Cat Street
YOYOGI STADIUM (1964 OLYMPICS)
SHIBUYA

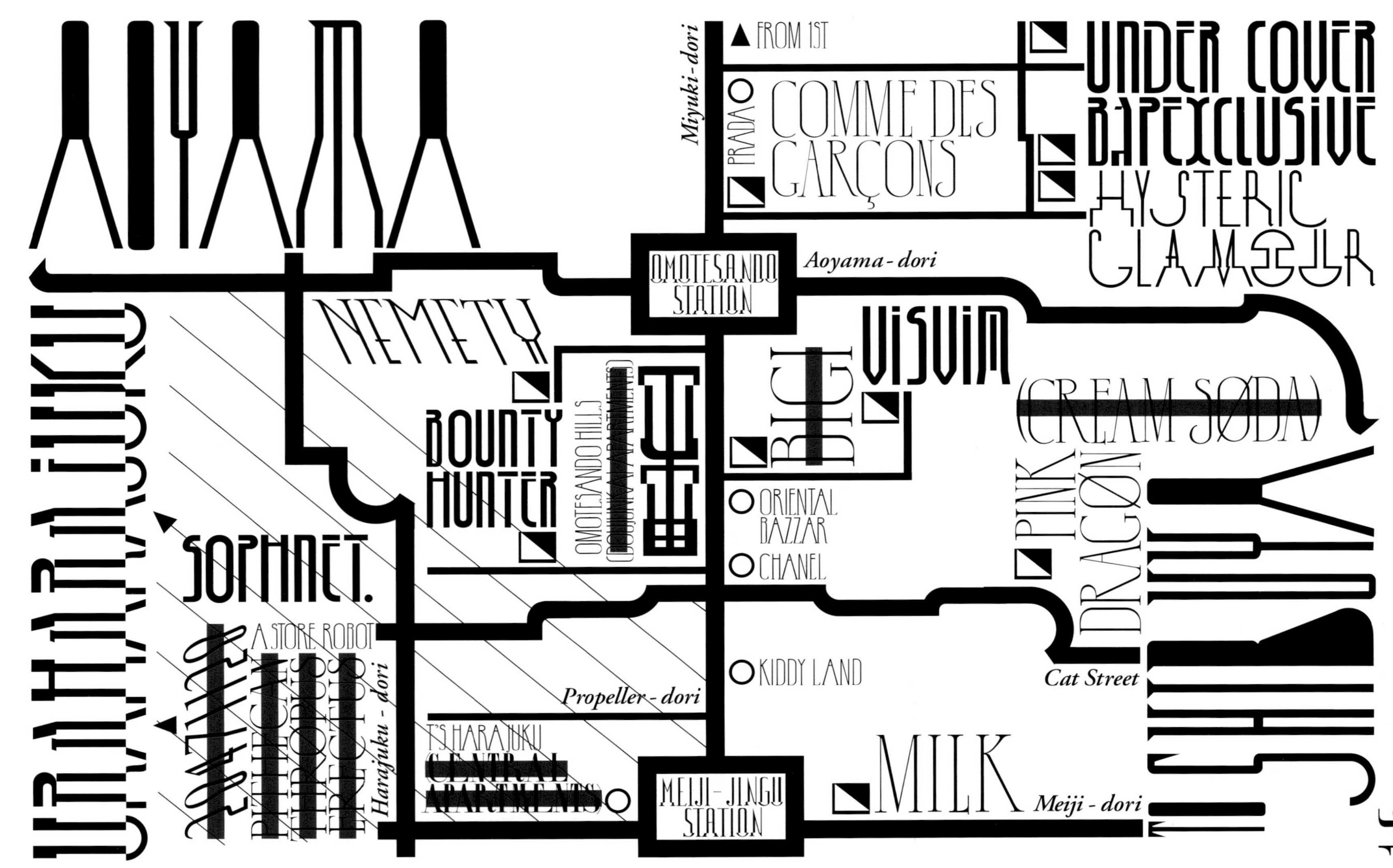
URAHARAJUKU
AOYAMA
SOPHNET.
A STORE ROBOT
PITHECANTHROPUS ERECTUS
Harajuku - dori
NEMETH
BOUNTY HUNTER
T'S HARAJUKU
Propeller - dori
OMOTESANDO HILLS
(DOUJUNKAI APARTMENTS)
MEIJI-JINGU STATION
OMOTESANDO STATION
Miyuki-dori
KIDDY LAND
CHANEL
ORIENTAL BAZZAR
BIGI
PRADA
FROM 1ST
COMME DES GARÇONS
Aoyama-dori
VISVIM
MILK
PINK DRAGON
CREAM SODA
Meiji - dori
Cat Street
UNDERCOVER
BAPEXCLUSIVE
HYSTERIC GLAMOUR
SHIBUYA

Cat Street

Snaking a curvy path that runs basically parallel to Meiji-dori, Cat Street stretches from Shibuya to the northernmost end of the Harajuku district. Real estate used to cost less on Cat Street, allowing smaller, lesser-known brands and boutiques to establish a foothold near the center of the Harajuku scene. However, as these stores thrived, the area developed an insider-hip cachet that has drawn the attention of larger enterprises. As more established stores have moved in, they have begun erecting showcase buildings and—as on Omotesando—driving up prices. A prime example is a furniture store designed by Tadao Ando.

URA-HARA

This mire of alleyways is the cradle of modern Japanese fashion, first adopted by young designers lured by inexpensive rent. These creators would come to be Mansion Makers in the early 1970s. "Mansion" in this case is a misnomer, meaning an apartment building built with cement. Now the area is overrun with little shops and cafés, and the district surrounding the street has become known as Ura-Hara (a shorthand colloquialism meaning "the backstreets of Harajuku").

Meiji-dori

Running parallel to the Yamanote line between Harajuku and Shibuya, Meiji-dori is the main pedestrian artery connecting the two shopping zones. Lined with tiny shops, the little streets that radiate out from this main drag are comparable to London's Kings Road. Palais France, which was at the corner of Takeshita-dori and Meiji-dori, was the first building in the area to house luxury boutiques back in the early 1970s. The intersection of Meiji-dori and Omotesando, anchored by the Laforet shopping complex, is the nerve center of all Harajuku fashion. Snap-shooters and fashion's cool hunters alike consider this spot prime hunting ground.

Omotesando

Urban legend has it that this once sleepy, tree-lined street was used as a temporary landing strip for the American military during World War II. Though that is totally untrue, Omotesando has had quite an important role in the history of Harajuku fashion. Omotesando, the spine of Harajuku, runs from Meiji Jingu to Aoyama-dori. From the early 1980s to 2000, it was a "Pedestrian Paradise" on Sundays when the street was closed to cars and populated by an assortment of rockabilly dancers, amateur vocalists, craftspeople, and fashionable folk. While Omotesando is still a gathering spot for youth, several dramatic changes have transformed it into another place to shop for generic, international luxury brands. Much-adored as the site of Harajuku's early days of youth culture and fashion, Doujunkai Apartments was torn down to make room for the Omotesando Hills shopping complex.

KIDDY LAND

Kiddy Land is five floors of everything you expect Japan to be. Overflowing with toys, licensed character goods, stationery, and various collectibles, Kiddy Land is often filled with middle-aged O.L.s (office ladies), tourists, and the occasional celebrity. Anyone who stops in Tokyo, however brief the trip, makes a point to pop by. Opening its doors in 1950, Kiddy Land was originally the Tokyo branch of the Hashidate bookstore. Quick to see that business should be aimed at the local residents at the time—the soldiers and families from the American army base Washington Heights—the store started stocking Japanese novelty and souvenir gifts. They eventually added American novelty goods like dolls and games not found in Japan, attracting Japanese customers as well. Situated in the same location for the last sixty years, it is the meeting ground between hip Harajuku and the luxe Aoyama district.

THE RØØTS HARAJUK

I have always believed that for a woman to become beautiful, it all depends on having a good environment. With the change in a woman's style or fashion, the city changes, too. With that in mind, I opened my boutique on Omotesando in Harajuku and in the Aoyama district to create the new face of beauty—first with the intent of changing Tokyo, and then the world.

—Shu Uemura

THE RØØTS

HARAJUKU

HARAJUKU'S START

The røøts of Tokyo's Street Fashion Scene

by Takeji Hirakawa

The transformation of Harajuku into the iconic fashion district we know it as today began after the end of World War II. I was born in Osaka in 1945, six months before the end of the war. The first time I saw Harajuku was in 1955, when I was ten years old. I remember it took seventeen or eighteen hours to travel from Osaka to Tokyo on a steam-powered train. Now it seems so simple to make the journey on the Shinkansen, but after the war many of the fruits of Japan's industrialization had not yet come about, and domestic travel was still quite an ordeal, requiring money, time, and courage. I recall touring Tokyo on the Hato sightseeing bus, and faintly remember Harajuku as a broad boulevard with Keyaki trees—upscale and modern compared to where I lived.

Shortly after I was born, lodgings for U.S. commissioned officers and their families, Washington Heights, were built in Harajuku, south of the Meiji Jingu, on a vacant lot that previously had been used for military drills. The completion of Washington Heights and the introduction of foreign families to the area planted the seeds of a sophisticated, international district that had never before existed in Japan. At that time—the lean years after the war—most Japanese people had no experience with Western culture, fashions, or lifestyles. But the young Japanese of Harajuku, because they were living in close proximity with the American families in Washington Heights and surrounding areas, were ahead of the curve, and their envy of the Westerners' cool styles seeped into their dreams and ambitions, laying the roots for the Harajuku of today.

このワシントンハイツの登場と
そこに住んだアメリカ軍将校
家族たちが実は、この原宿という街を
何かしらそれまでの日本には無い
モダーンでハイカラな雰囲気と
センスが感じられインターナショナルな
魅力ある街のルーツ&メモリアルを
インキュベーションし始めた
存在となった。

In 1958 Harajuku took a step closer to its modern, international, and stylish self with the construction of Central Apartments, soon to be occupied by the living and working spaces of fashion designers, models, photographers, and graphic designers (now the site of T's Harajuku, which includes a multifloor Gap shop). In 1964, the Summer Olympics opened in Tokyo. The main arena (the Olympic Indoor Football Stadium, designed by architect Kenzo Tange) was built next to the vacant Yoyogi military drill field and what was once Washington Heights, which became the Olympic Village. A distinct "Harajuku" feel was born as the first boutiques, late-night restaurants, and cafés opened in the area.

The completion of Washington Heights and the introduction of foreign families to the area planted the seeds of a sophisticated, international district that had never before existed in Japan.

After the Olympics, the young people who hung out in Harajuku—called the *Harajuku-zoku* (Harajuku tribe)—began to develop a unique sensibility and stylishness that distinguished them from groups hanging out in Tokyo's other shopping areas, such as Ginza, which was popular with the *Miyuki-zoku* (Miyuki is the name of a street in Ginza). The area, because of the density of like-minded creators working there, became known as the place to be for those seeking a shortcut to the fashion world. Clothing designers, models, stylists, hair and makeup artists, and anyone else who wanted to become part of Japan's fashion industry flocked to Harajuku. Harajuku offered something not found elsewhere in Tokyo. It was this charged atmosphere that so mesmerized the young men and women.

Toward the end of the 1970s I was an occasional contributing writer to *Ryuko-Tsushin,* one of the leading Japanese fashion magazines. I recall a popular manual of the time, titled something like "How to Succeed in the Fashion Business," which advised the hopeful to rent a small room in an inexpensive apartment block in the backstreets of Harajuku (in the area now known as Ura-Hara), set up an atelier, and start working. Young designers' collections were at least one-third copies of that season's international designs, which were typically highly sought after in the domestic market. Easily mistaken for overseas brands, the collections would then be sold wholesale to small shops. Another route was for designers to rent cheap commercial space in Takeshita-dori and open their own retail shops—a strategy now considered a good method for selling independent designs. Here, selling directly to consumers, designers could test and produce more of the items that sold well. By exhibiting new collections four to five times per year

この原宿と言う街が持っている
もう一つの可能性は
『ファッション業界人』になれる
という可能性である。

for several years, they might begin to see a profit, which they might then use to buy editorial coverage in a fashion magazine—a form of advertising known as a "tie-up." (I remember nominal rates for advertising at the time were about U.S. $1,000 for a full two-page spread, which was often negotiated down to about half-price.) Once a designer's clothes became known through the power of the magazine's image, the designer could "talk up" (or even fabricate) his or her history and background to further promote the designs, which would help drive sales.

Getting this far was halfway to success, and at this point, a designer might feel that his or her brand had arrived on the fashion scene. The next step would be to open a shop in Laforet or another building with numerous fashion tenants—or better still, open a street-level, stand-alone shop—then establish a company and grow the business, expanding distribution throughout the country. This is still the path most frequently traveled by those seeking success in the fashion industry in Japan.

In the 1960s and 1970s property values in Harajuku were cheaper than in surrounding districts, allowing designers to consolidate their work and sales in one location and maintain a level of creative independence otherwise unavailable to them. They worked out of inexpensive home offices with the support of tiny staffs. This small-scale production with limited lot size and outlay allowed the designers to limit their production to only that which interested them. An integral part of the fashion industry of the time, these small home-based designers came to be known as "Mansion Makers." (An apartment building is referred to as a "mansion" in Japan. Such misnomers are fairly common with appropriations of English into Japanese.) Since the late 1960s, brands such as Hitomi Okawa's Milk, Mitsuhiro Matsuda's Nicole, Kansai Yamamoto, Comme des Garçons, and Yohji Yamamoto's Y's all started out in this way in Harajuku. Issey Miyake, however, predated the Mansion Makers. By the 1960s the Issey Miyake brand had already begun working with licensing, and it enjoyed distribution through Seibu department stores and the backing of the textile manufacturer Toray Industries.

The area, because of the density of like-minded creators working there, became known as the place to be for those seeking a shortcut to the fashion world.

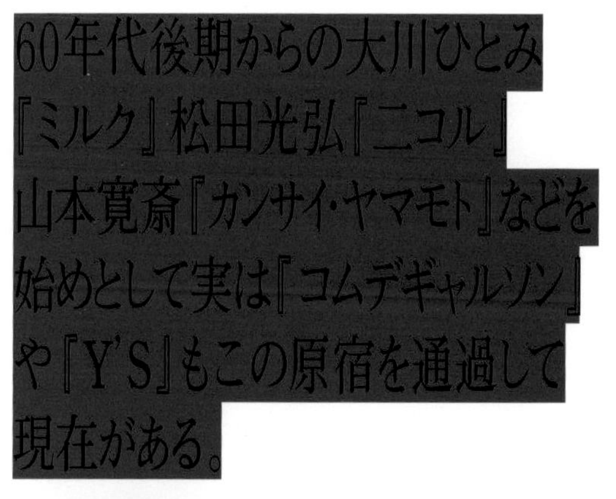

The first media publication to celebrate these designers was the magazine *An An,* launched in 1971, followed by *Non No,* which came out later that same year. Both included special features on Harajuku in every issue, helping establish the area's iconic image as the locus of youth fashion and aspirations. The opening in 1978 of Laforet, with its alternative selection of new designers, further focused media attention on the neighborhood, contributing to the transformation of Harajuku (and specifically Laforet) into the epicenter of the young fashion industry. As Harajuku boomed, with growing numbers of young designers, manufacturers, and retail outlets for this new fashion scene, the small labels grew into what became known as Designer Character (DC) brands by the mid-1980s.

Although the recent rise in property values and the arrival of many large, international designer boutiques such as Ralph Lauren, Christian Dior, and Chanel have begun to force out some smaller boutiques and individual designer shops and heralded the arrival of large-scale materialism, Harajuku still maintains its unique, close-knit neighborhood feel, something that is extremely unusual for a Japanese city. Its identity is still all about selling Japan's modern culture, its trends, its stylishness, and a certain kind of dream—a sense of possibility. In Harajuku, you can feel the possibility of buying your dream, of holding it in your hand.

Since the late 1960s, brands such as Hitomi Okawa's Milk, Mitsuhiro Matsuda's Nicole, Kansai Yamamoto, Comme des Garçons, and Yohji Yamamoto's Y's all started out in Harajuku.

CENTRAL APARTMENTS

セントラル アパートメント

The Central Apartments complex served as a nexus of creativity in the late 1960s and 1970s. It was home to many of the key players who would later emerge as major forces in Japanese fashion, design, art, photography, music, and new advertising. They hung out at Café Leon, on the building's ground floor. Japan's first boutique, Mademoiselle Non Non, opened on the first floor of Central Apartments in 1964. Milk would open right next door in 1970.

Yacco Takahashi, a freelancer for a small advertising office in Central Apartments, was the first professional stylist to work in Japan. She moved easily between the worlds of fashion, music, and advertising, and was as familiar with the New York–based editorial offices of magazines such as *Harper's Bazaar* as she was with cutting-edge fashion in Central Apartments. Takahashi had entrée into alluring international scenes that were seemingly inaccessible to most Japanese, quickly becoming legendary among her countrymen. Japanese designers visiting the States used her as their point person, receiving advice and contacts to help further their efforts.

Takahashi often worked with designer Kansai Yamamoto, whose atelier was just down the road from Central Apartments. Together they traveled to the U.K. to check out Swinging London. Through the model Tina Lutz (before she became fashion icon Tina Chow), Takahashi and Yamamoto met Michael Chow, of Mr. Chow restaurant fame. In 1971, with Chow's help, Yamamoto became the first Japanese designer to show in London. His first collection featured colorful, busy prints modeled after traditional Japanese styles, including work wear and kabuki costumes. A real showman, Yamamoto put together a theatrical extravaganza that featured Japanese rock band Carol along with a cast numbering into the hundreds. It was at this landmark show that David Bowie first saw Yamamoto's designs, and he later borrowed wardrobe from this show for his performance at Radio City Music Hall. When Bowie as Ziggy Stardust donned Yamamoto's cosmic designs, he cemented his love affair with Japan and rocketed Japanese design further into the space-age future.

Masayoshi Sukita, the grandfather of Japanese music photography, also had a small office in Central Apartments, and also worked with Takahashi. He frequently photographed foreign musicians visiting Japan, most notably T. Rex, David Bowie, and Iggy Pop. As part of T. Rex's 1972 Japan tour, Sukita and Takahashi organized a T. Rex exhibition and Marc Bolan look-alike contest. Sukita was also hired to be Bowie's official photographer for his Japanese tour in 1973, the start of their ongoing professional relationship.

In 1977, Bowie asked Sukita, with only a day's notice, to photograph him and Iggy Pop, and to provide leather jackets for the shoot. Takahashi picked the musicians up from the Imperial Hotel, gave them an impromptu tour of Tokyo's back streets, and then took them to Harajuku Studio, a rinky-dink venue where Sukita was waiting for them. He had only one hour to shoot both musicians. Sukita started with Bowie, who played with layering jackets during the shoot, finally settling on one; Pop danced around a bit, and the session was over. A few months later, Bowie's record company contacted Sukita for permission to use the photographs from that Tokyo session. These images are featured on the covers of Bowie's *Heroes* and Iggy Pop's *Party* albums.

David Bowie, T. Rex, and Iggy Pop photographed by Masayoshi Sukita in Harajuku, posing with stylist Yacco Takahashi and working with designer Kansai Yamamoto (kneeling).

BIGI
ビギ

Designer Takeo Kikuchi got his start working as a tailor for order-made clothes in the luxury, straightlaced world of Tokyo's Ginza district. Europe's elegance and long-established tradition of clothing making were important to Kikuchi, as was the explosive youth culture he was seeing, particularly in London. Influenced by Swinging London and Biba (a key brand and lifestyle department store for glamorizing streetwear), Kikuchi came to Harajuku in 1971 to launch his womenswear line Bigi. His spacious boutique on Omotesando (now Paul Stuart) was one of the first boutiques in the area, along with Milk and Mademoiselle Non Non. His fashion helped bring London Glam to Tokyo and brush aside American styles that were previously popular. In 1975 he started Men's Bigi, which was a reflection of his own personal penchant for dandified suits and expertly cut leisurewear—a look that would become his trademark. Photographs of his clothes as shot by fine-art photographer Shoji Ueda (seen here) are inseparable from the brand's image. Bigi enjoyed great commercial success, along with many other domestic brands during the DC and economic boom of the 1980s, becoming the first Japanese brand to open a menswear boutique in Paris. Kikuchi's empire became the Bigi Group, a stable of successful brands. In 1984 Kikuchi sold the Bigi Group to form his own eponymous label, with "London Pop" as its theme label, through apparel company giant World. In 2004, he handed over the design reins and rolls out his own blend of cool gents' style in Omotesando today.

Images from the catalogue "Men's Bigi Takeo Kikuchi Autumn & Winter Collection 83–84," photographed by Shoji Ueda.

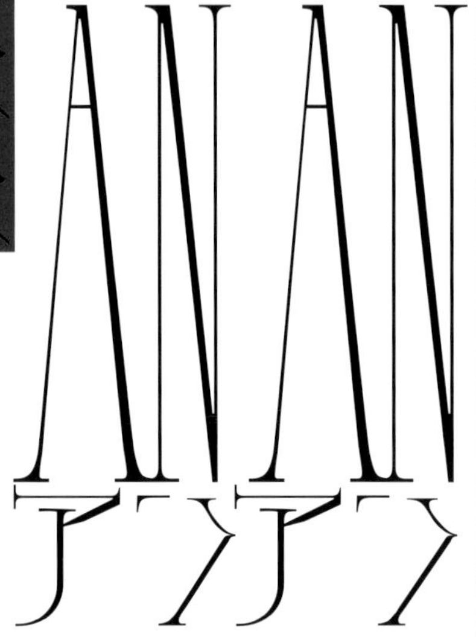

Launched in 1970 and still going strong today, *An An* was the first Japanese fashion magazine to focus on the young designers emerging out of Harajuku. Featuring brands such as Comme des Garçons, Milk, and Kaneko Isao, *An An* reveled in the scenesters, fashionistas, and other rising stars of Japan's emerging fashion and youth culture scenes. This was a sharp contrast to the fashion magazines in the market until then, like *Dressmaking, Fukuso,* and *So-En,* which included actual dress patterns and were geared for readers poised with needle and thread. An issue of *An An* might include profiles of Shuji Terayama's avant-garde theater, moody illustrations by Akira Uno, and new fashions by designer Junko Koshino alongside photo stories featuring artistic nudes by the photographer Kishin Shinoyama. Though foreign fashion was also represented in each issue through the inclusion of pages from French *Elle,* it was *An An*'s primarily Japanese slant, its fresh art direction by Seiichi Horiuchi, and fashion photography by Saburo Tatsuki that combined to create a new visual language for Japanese fashion. In Saburo's efforts to create "something strange, but cute," as he described his photographic style, he got the models to move in an expressive, freestyle manner. Saburo's work had a charm similar to the work of Britain's revolutionary fashion photographer David Bailey, though Saburo hadn't been exposed to Bailey's work. As he said, "If the girl couldn't move, I knew I was in trouble and I would have to go after something more orthodox. Trying for a shot that might appear in *Vogue* could have been easier, but that was not what I was after." (Japanese fashion fans of the time were dedicated readers of French *Vogue*.)

An An further challenged traditional Japanese culture by featuring mixed-race models. In such a monoethnic

外苑東通

Mademoiselle
NON NON

country, the inclusion of Japanese as well as half-Japanese models countered the racial xenophobia prevalent throughout Japan's history. One such model, Yuri Kaneko (née Tachikawa), was featured on numerous covers. *An An*'s second issue featured the editorial "Yuri in Venice," the first fashion shoot done abroad by a Japanese fashion magazine. Tachikawa's regular appearance in *An An* was the beginning of what would become standard practice in the world of Japanese fashion magazines: linking certain models to a magazine's identity.

Pages 30–33: Model Yuri Kaneko, photographed by Saburo Tatsuki for magazine covers and fashion editorials for *An An*.

RYUKO TSUSHIN

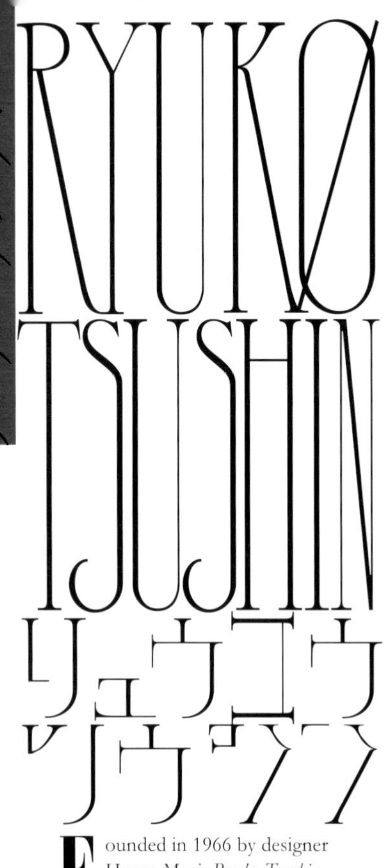

リュウコウツウシン

Founded in 1966 by designer Hanae Mori, *Ryuko-Tsushin* (Trend Communique) was initially created as an in-store gift (with purchase), available at Mori's boutique on Omotesando. Packed with features of foreign fashion news and a burgeoning creative youth scene, *Ryu-Tsu* was a fashion and culture bible for the fashion industry. By 1970, the magazine became available in bookstores sporting a new logo and new art direction by Ikko Tanaka (who had also done design work for Issey Miyake). The models used for photo shoots were almost exclusively foreign. This helped create a sense of fantasy that distinguished it from its domestic competitor *An An,* which primarily used Japanese or part-Japanese models. Apart from its sharp eye for emerging fashion designers, art direction by Tadanori Yokoo (from 1976), photography by Jumonji Bishin, and occasional contributions by art director Eiko Ishioka each helped give the magazine its edgy incarnation that remains its legacy. A year before Iman became *Vogue*'s first black cover model, she was featured on the January 1978 cover of *Ryu-Tsu* with the title "The Now Girl." Over the years, as *An An* became more commercial, branching out to a growing fashion-hungry mainstream, *Ryu-Tsu* stayed dedicated to experimentation and emerging talent. In 2006, however, market pressures forced the magazine to also pursue a more commercially minded path.

流行通信 1

ASHION NEWS 1978 JAN. NO.167

Covers from the magazine *Ryuko-Tsushin* in the 1970s.

特集=いまの女イマン

MILK

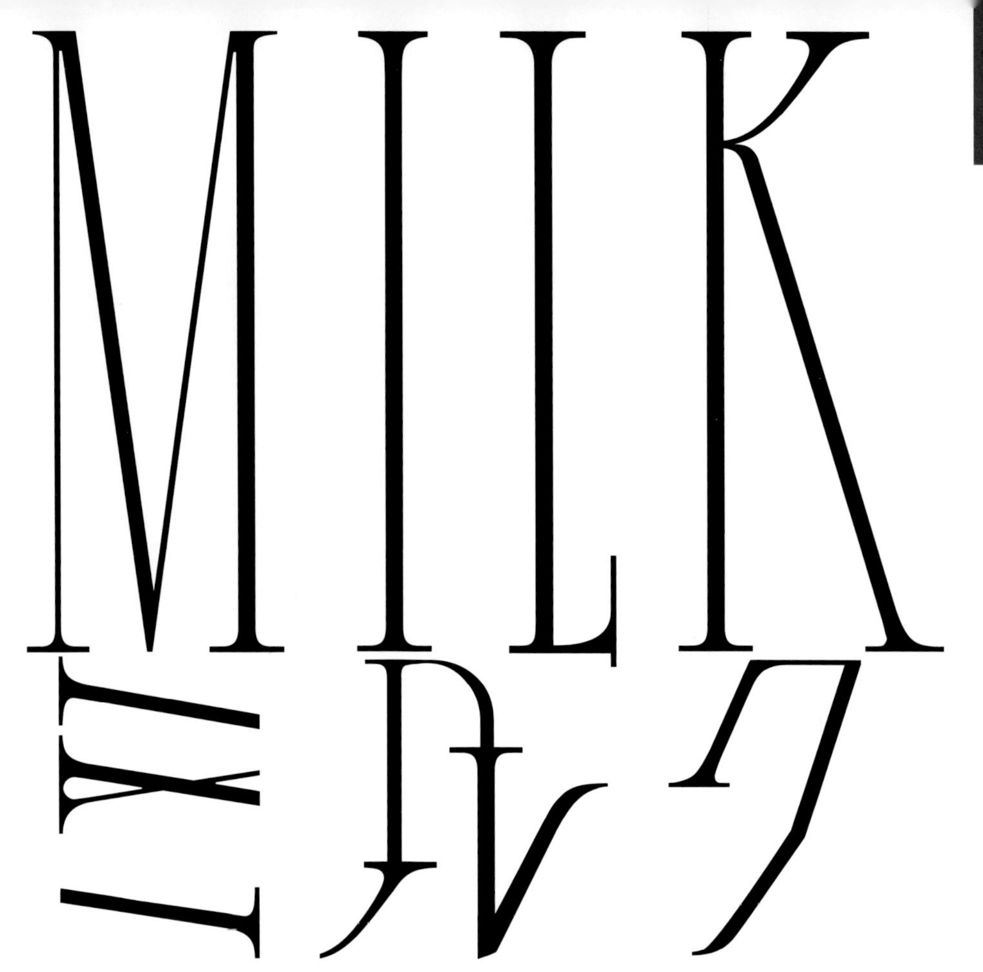

Buyer, promoter, talent scout, and party girl, Hitomi Okawa might be called the Muse of Harajuku. One of the first of the new wave of designers to emerge in Harajuku in the 1960s, she opened her shop Milk in 1970. Originally an alleyway next to Central Apartments, it was so small that if you adjusted your sunglasses or blinked at the moment you walked by, you'd miss it.

Okawa quickly became a key player. It seems as if everyone who passed through Tokyo came to know her. Designers from Fiorucci, Vivienne Westwood, and Stephen Jones hung out in her shop when they came to town. John Lennon and David Bowie were regular customers. A whole generation of Harajuku's cutting-edge young designers has some connection to Milk. Comme des Garçons was first sold in Milk's stall. Milk is also regarded as the godmother of Ura-Hara, a newly defined sub-district within Harajuku known for its streetwear designers. The central figures of Ura-Hara—Hiroshi Fujiwara, Nigo of A Bathing Ape, and Jonio of UNDER COVER—all got DJ gigs and introductions to magazine editors with Okawa's help (she thought they were "cute kids" and was happy to help them out). Fujiwara credits her with his success. What he later went on to do as a brand consultant and gateway to foreign cultures, she had already achieved through her store.

Milk took in all of fashion's disparate parts and made its own combination of looks, creating something entirely new. Before Milk, no one would ever say that punk is cute. But in Okawa's hands, it really was. She took tracksuits from the States and punk fashions from the U.K., redesigned them to fit smaller Japanese bodies and twisted them into something entirely new and of the moment. For her, as for other designers making forays abroad from Harajuku, the world became one giant jumble sale providing inspiration for imaginative new styles.

Since childhood, she knew she wanted to "do something artistic, like fashion." Just after high school, she traveled to London, where she "saw the light": "The parties, the lifestyle . . . London was the shit. It was all about street fashion. All of this. This is for me!" She thought, "How can I be a part of this in Japan?" With a three-month commitment of support from her parents, she launched her shop; some thirty-odd years later, she's still at it, right in the middle of the party, surrounded by all the coolest kids.

When Okawa started out she didn't know the first thing about designing or making clothes, figuring it out as she went along. Milk garments were made from surplus military fabric and the coarse, industrial material used for workers' clothes. She was also one of the first people to make designer T-shirts in Harajuku—a challenge to the suddenly retrograde, Ivy League cardigans-and-slacks-with-penny-loafers style favored in Ginza, another key shopping center in Tokyo. Right from the beginning, she had her finger on the pulse: Kids in Harajuku wanted streetwear, and Milk designs sold out as soon as they hit the racks. "It wouldn't have worked anywhere else," she says. "It was Harajuku, the people there being that cool . . . [The feeling] that new things could become a business was because of Harajuku."

In the 1980s she created antithetical styles to the looks then being designed for the newly independent working woman by Comme des Garçons and Yohji Yamamoto in Japan and Donna Karan in the West. Milk clothes were—and continue to be—girly, romantic, and feminine, but not sexual. All these elements are the base for what would later become *kawaii* culture. Milk was for party girls who wanted to feel like princesses, be cute, and go out with cute guys. After thirty years, Milk is still deeply committed to what is new, following what she feels, and making things that kids want to wear. The brand projects positivity and fun.

Page 36: Shop staff outside main store on Meiji-dori. *Right:* Images from Milk's self-produced magazine *Milk Bar*, 1996-2001. *Opposite:* Shop staff from Milk Boy, 2007.

I went to Harajuku on my first visit to Japan in 1984. I was part of a fashion show called London Goes to Tokyo, which was held at the Hanae Mori Fashion Foundation on Omotesando. This show highlighted the important young London designers of the day: Body Map, Leigh Bowery, Culture Shock, Richmond Cornejo, and myself. Just down the street lived and worked my only Japanese friend, Hitomi Okawa, of the shop Milk. I had met Hitomi at the Blitz Club in London a few years earlier and two of my London club friends, Lee Sheldrick and Stephen Linard, were working for her as designers. Milk had a near mythical status. We knew that the shop was the first in the world to stock Comme des Garçons, but it also sold the line Milk Boy, which at that time on the London Club scene was the most exclusive and elusive designer label. On that first trip, Hitomi showed me around Harajuku: the **gaijins** ***at Café de Rope; Oriental Bazaar; the jiving Teddy Boys in Yoyogi Park; the sweet schoolgirls on Takeshita-dori transforming themselves into fashion icons; and my personal favorite, the toyshop Kiddy Land. Kiddy Land seemed to blend the traditional culture of Japan with hi n-r-g of fluorescent pink plastic to a Blade Runner-esque level—and it still does today. For me, Harajuku is not about shopping or fashion, (it is just as much about a ¥100 shop as Louis Vuitton), but one of the few places in Japan where young people can have a sense of freedom and express themselves through clothes.***

—Stephen Jones

ーム・ソーダ物語
Cream Soda
TEDDY B
ロックンロール・バイ
TEMMYE
VIVIENNE
TEMMYE
19 50
CREAM SODA
Cream Soda
MODERN CLASSIC B2F
STREET FASHION B2F
PINK DRAGON
CREAM SODA
CREAM SODA
TOO FAST TO LIVE TOO YOUNG TO DIE
CREAM SODA
TO LIVE TO DIE
IT'S SO NEW! IT'S SO MODERN! IT'S SO DIFFERENT!
PINK
DRAGON
NOW can be YOURS!
TOKYO FUN-FUN SOUVENIR
TOO FAST TO LIVE
CREAM SO
TOKYO. SAPPORO. KYO
HARAJUKU TOKYO
CREAM SODA
TOO FAST TO LIVE TOO YOUNG TO DIE
JAPAN
CREAM SODA
EVERYTHING BEGINS AT CAT STREET
PINK
DRAGON
TEMMYE

CREAM SODA & BLACK CATS

クリームソーダアンドブラックキャッツ

Cream Soda owner Masayuki Yamazaki's rock-and-roll fantasies began not in Harajuku, but across town in the nightlife district of Shinjuku. It was in Shinjuku in 1968 that he opened Kaijin Niju Menso (The Mysterious Man with Twenty Faces—named after the Edogawa Rampo story), a bad-boy bar that attracted bikers, nationalists, and other grunge characters. Despite the bar's locals-only atmosphere, Takeo Kikuchi, Kansai Yamamoto, and a few other fashion rebels occasionally braved the four dark flights up to ring the buzzer. Inside, the bar was styled to match Yamazaki's impression of America as seen through early Elvis Presley movies: black-painted walls, black leather jackets, black sunglasses. Yamazaki spun American-style rock and rhythm & blues from the 1950s and 1960s—then a rarity in Japan—and the Japanese rock band Carol provided live music. One-hundred-fifty rockers could pack onto the club's dance floor, and even pushed into the kitchen and toilet to catch the live concerts.

The music scene in the early 1970s in Harajuku was much more staid and gently nostalgic, typified by the folk music that dominated clubs like Penny Lane. In 1974, Yamazaki (or "Yama-chan," as he was universally known) opened a coalmine-themed bar in Harajuku called King Kong. The darkness of the venue, punctured only by small lights, probably was the basis for the theme. It was a fortuitous location. Surpassing Shinjuku, Harajuku was becoming the center of the new Japanese youth culture, which included the disaffected children of increasingly work-fixated salarymen. Bikers and working-class kids from Tokyo and surrounding areas such as Kanagawa, Chiba, and Saitama came to Harajuku to hang out. Sundays saw the greatest concentration of these kids, who spent the day on Omotesando.

Wanting to introduce his customers to his own version of a 1950s retro American style, Yamazaki launched the Cream Soda label in 1976. For research, Yamazaki went not to America but to London, where the Teds, Rockers, and Mods had adopted aspects of American rock and biker culture and turned the bad-boy, leather look into a fashion statement. Vivienne Lynn, Yamazaki's half-Japanese, half-British fashion-model girlfriend, also influenced his sense of style (the two met while she was on a shoot in Tokyo for Shiseido). Lynn was a central figure in the London fashion scene at the time and one of the biggest models of the 1970s, regularly working with Biba, Zandra Rhodes, and Vivienne Westwood. She provided Yamazaki entrée into London's fashion world.

Cream Soda was an immediate success—the first collection sold out in two weeks. At the time, Japanese fashion was still largely an exercise in copying collections from Paris, and, unlike Yamazaki, most designers had attended design school. Cream Soda was totally different from what anyone else was doing in Japanese design at the time—different enough that it was largely ignored by fashion and culture magazines.

Yamazaki distributed Cream Soda through a highly selective nightclub-like shop called Pink Dragon that allowed only a select few through its doors. Despite (or because of) this, the brand became hotly coveted. Its most popular item was a leopard-print wallet with a Cream Soda tag. (The store also sold tons of pomade.) Yamazaki himself was no more accessible than his clothing line. He was a mystery man who seldom appeared in public. For him, all his work was about the music, not the clothes or the brand or his reputation as a "designer." Rock and roll was what he sold—the lifestyle and its dangerous image. But still, the Cream Soda look quickly became pure fashion.

In 1978 Garage Paradise Tokyo opened in Harajuku. It was a pioneering lifestyle store offering mid-century American furniture and rocker gear, influenced by the vintage American clothing store Paradise Garage in London, which hosted Vivienne Westwood and Malcolm McLaren's Let It Rock boutique. The rock and roll style had put down roots in Japan, and with the opening of this store it was no longer dependent on Yamazaki and Cream Soda. He shuttered Pink Dragon and closed Cream Soda in that same year.

What next to do but to start a band? On a whim, Yamazaki and the guys in his shop formed the Black Cats, who played (guess what?) American-style roots rockabilly and became a best-selling Japanese act in Japan for Victor records. Like the Plastics, they were a flagship Harajuku band, and, despite the genre of their music, they were likewise swept up in the new wave scene. The Black Cats were invited to open for the Go-Go's on their West Coast tour in 1982 after the band caught Yamazaki's group performing at L.A.'s China Club. It was also at the China Club that the Black Cats met Timothy Leary, when he approached the band—holding a Cream Soda book Yamazaki had published in Japan—to get an autograph. "Leary likes you a lot," someone told Yamazaki. "Tomorrow you can get great LSD!" Joe Strummer and the rest of The Clash were official fan club members as well.

Pages 40–41: Collage of images generated for the brand Cream Soda. *Below:* Near Jingu Bridge, "The Rollers," who adopted the Cream Soda look. *Opposite:* Imagery from Cream Soda's owner Yama-chan and Black Cats.

原宿
BLACK CATS
CREAM SODA RECORD®
BLACK SUNPLAZ
LACK CATS
19
82
S.A TOUR

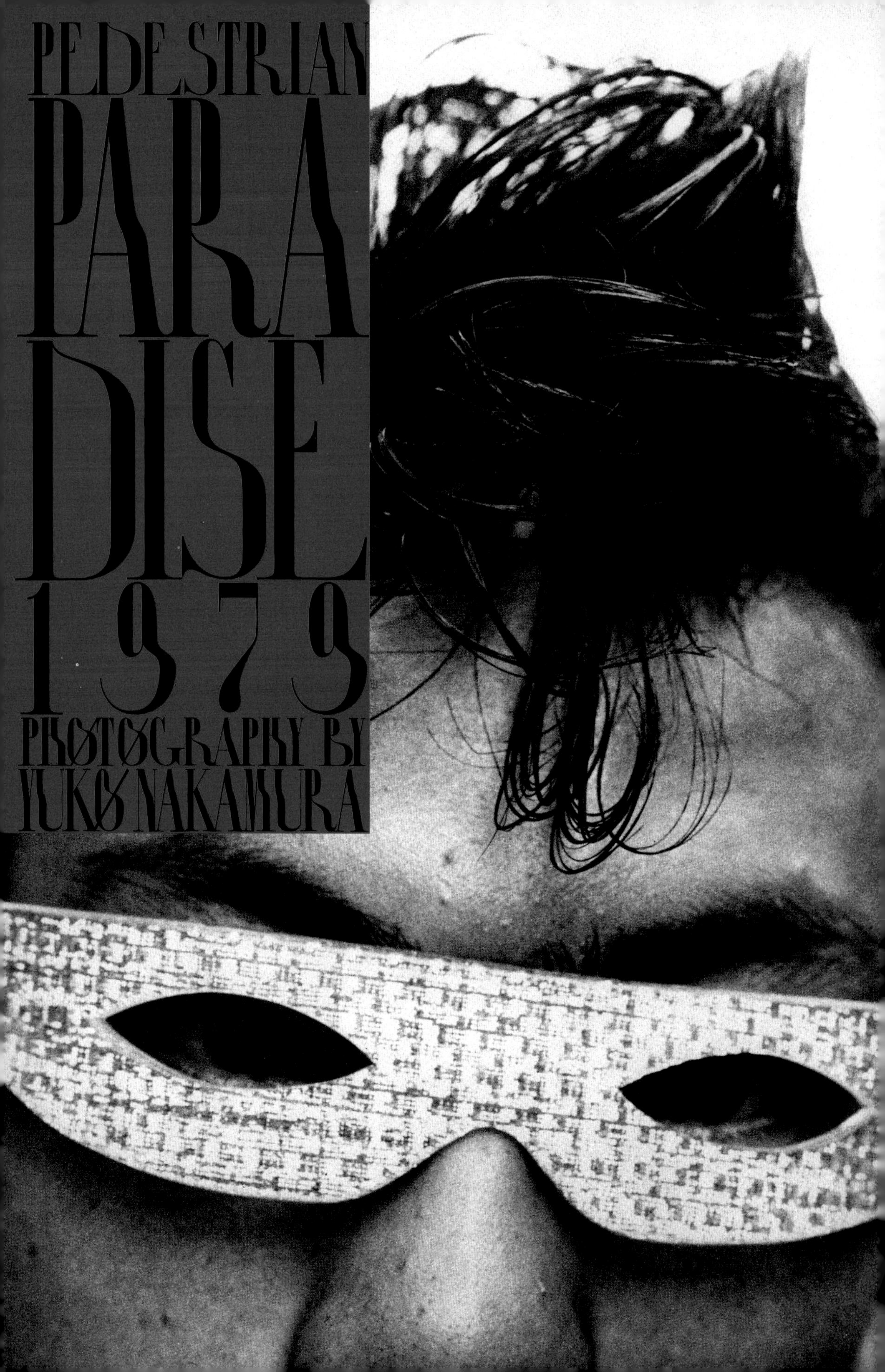
PEDESTRIAN
PARA
DISE
1979
PHOTOGRAPHY BY
YUKO NAKAMURA

From the late 1970s to 2000, Harajuku's main drag was closed to traffic every Sunday, making an ad-hoc stage, catwalk, bazaar, street boutique, and concert hall. This "Pedestrian Paradise" was called *Hokoten* in Japanese.

岩崎

SEX PISTOLS
NEVER MIND THE BOLLOCKS

Early photographs of the Plastics during their punk phase, circa 1978. Kaoru Ijima, who was just starting his career at the time, became their unofficial official photographer, and also toured with them in the States. These images are from shows at Tsubaki House, a trendy “live house” in Shinjuku.

THE PLASTICS & PITHECAN THRØPUS ERECTUS

ザ プラスティックス アンド ピテカン トロプス エレクトス

From the mid-1970s to the early 1980s, Harajuku's music and fashion scenes shifted apace with new movements from the West, from glam to punk to new wave to hip-hop. The Plastics, a "fashion concept" band, embodied it all, transforming both their music and image and staying cutting-edge. The band lasted from 1975 to 1981, and went from shiny to punky to happy to funky (in its later incarnation as Melon). Their first single, "Copy" b/w "Robot," was released on the none-cooler-than tastemaker U.K. label Rough Trade. The key members of the band—Masuhide Sakuma (keyboards, guitar, and bass), Hajime Tachibana (guitar and vocals), Takemi Shima (rhythm box), Toshio Nakanishi (guitar and vocals), and Chica Sato (lead vocals)—all moved on to other projects that continued to be influential in shaping music and culture. Sakuma was the producer for X JAPAN and GLAY. Tachibana launched a career as an artist and graphic designer. Shima became a commercial songwriter. And Nakanishi and Sato ruled the Tokyo club and fashion scenes as trendsetters responsible for bringing British and American new wave, graffiti, and hip-hop to Japan.

The Plastics' first gig in 1977 was at the Mominoki House, Tokyo's first health food restaurant, playing in a Roxy Music vein. In the same year, their friend, the designer Hiromichi Nakano, returned from London with a copy of the Sex Pistols' first single, "Anarchy in the U.K.," which led to the Plastics' transition to punk (Nakanishi and Sato in particular started sporting Vivienne Westwood's clothes).

Harajuku social life for them was centered around Café Leon, progressive boutique-and-lounge Chez Toi, and graphic designer and illustrator Pater Sato's studio (where Tachibana and Nakanishi worked as design assistants). As in London, the hip style in Tokyo was flashy and extreme—looking freaky for the sake of looking freaky. The Plastics usually met up at Chez Toi (just as the Sex Pistols had hung around Vivienne Westwood and Malcolm McLaren's shop Sex in London), where Shima was able to persuade the management to hire the über-stylish Chica Sato as a shop girl. The band virtually lived in bondage gear and primarily wore clothes from Vivienne Westwood's Pirates collection. "I looked great in it," recalls Sato.

When the Talking Heads came to Tokyo in 1981 in their minimal black jeans and T-shirts, the Plastics were impressed by this new look: the Heads looked like New York ninjas. Nakanishi and Tachibana were hired to design the Talking Heads' tour pamphlets. David Byrne liked the Plastics' sound, so he introduced the group to the B-52s' management; the Plastics were in new wave heaven. They were hired to tour the United States in 1981 with the Talking Heads, the B-52s, and the Ramones. Iggy Pop considered asking them to produce his forthcoming album. But at the end of the year, the band broke up. Nakanishi and Sato continued to perform together, calling themselves Melon.

In 1982, producer Moichi Kuwahara opened a club called Pithecan Thropus Erectus in Harajuku, just a few minutes' walk north of the station. A large, two-floor underground space, it was the first club to play rap in Japan. Hiroshi Fujiwara and Takagi Kan were on decks, and Melon played there regularly. The club was also a venue for art events and fashion shows. In 1982, artist Jean-Michel Basquiat accepted an invitation to put together an art exhibit. Basquiat knew Nakanishi from New York, and the two went club-hopping in Tokyo. After a fifteen-minute ride from Pithecan to Tokio in the Azabu district, the driver tried to give Basquiat back his 10,000-yen bill, saying it was too much for the fare. Basquiat tore it, leaving half on the seat of the taxi and running off to play in the Tokyo nightlife.

Imagine the surprise when acts like Talking Heads, Devo, and the B-52s first toured Japan, only to find that there was a somewhat similar but very Japanese scene that had emerged there almost simultaneously to ourselves. The Tokyo scene was focused around a ragtag band called Plastics, but also included fashion designers, illustrators, and graphic designers. The very name Plastics was a tip off: an ironic take on the common Western perception of Japanese products as being "plastic," and therefore inferior, copies of better made Western items. To some extent Plastics and their offspring Melon wanted to have it both ways—they acknowledged this perception, poked fun at it, and celebrated it all at the same time. In this sense they predicted the coming wave of Japanese product and invention that would soon engulf the world—the Walkman may have just been marketed in Japan, but the world didn't know about it yet. The complete 180-degree reversal of Western perception regarding Japanese exports had not yet happened. Soon Japanese products would be seen as the most well designed, prescient, and well made in the world, but not yet. The bands had philosophical ties to the do-it-yourself aesthetic common to the U.S. and U.K. punk bands, but they added more homemade spectacle than those bands usually did, and they actually did copy things they heard—chewed them up and regurgitated them as more peculiar and more Japanese. While Plastics was the Casio version of this—they were mostly electronic and synthesizer based—Melon added brass instruments, and absorbed dub, R & B and glam influences, making for a more eclectic performance. They added words to Bowie instrumentals and sang songs that celebrated a Harajuku club called Pithecan Thropus Erectus. To us Westerners the references were familiar, but the treatment of them was sometimes new. It was an era that was playful. Things hadn't solidified into genres and styles—everything was gloriously mixed up. It was colorful and pretty goofy. No one took too much of it seriously—though as with all play, there was indeed a serious statement being made deep down, that everyone could sense, but which was never articulated, as that would have spoiled the fun.

—David Byrne

Opposite: Plastics band member Toshio Nakanishi's notebooks from 1979–80 of their tour dates in New York. (Check out David Byrne and Siouxsie Sioux on the top and bottom right pages, respectively.) *Inset:* Drink ticket from Pithecan Thropus Erectus. *Below:* Plastics fans. *This page:* Hands down the most stylish girl in Harajuku, Chica Sato.

THE SCENE

PHOTOGRAPHY BY MARIPOL

Maripol was Madonna's first stylist and produced the film *Downtown 81* with Jean-Michel Basquiat in New York City. In these Polaroids taken on her 1979 research jaunt to Japan, she snapped Harajuku's Omotesando street scene (*opposite*), scene-makers Pater Sato and Benjamin Liu (*bottom left*), Plastics members Chica Sato and Toshio Nakanishi (*bottom right*), and this portrait of Sato (*top*).

Paris runway photographs of the S/S 1997 collection, Body Meets Dress, Dress Meets Body.

COMME DES GARÇONS

コムデギャルソン

Comme des Garçons has been a font of inspiration for the designers and creators working in Harajuku since the early 1970s. Even though the brand is not a Harajuku brand, its influence as a template-breaker and uncompromised creative force has broadly affected many sectors of fashion and design, including Harajuku designers, most of whom credit the label with paving the way. Its influence has been so pervasive that the label is now synonymous with contemporary fashion in Tokyo, as is its principal designer, art director, and corporate president, Rei Kawakubo.

Kawakubo is very much a product of her time—a generation that was born during the postwar recovery—and came of age in the 1960s and 1970s amidst the influx of foreign culture and creative energy creeping into Tokyo. In the late 1960s, Kawakubo worked as a freelance stylist for the few Japanese magazines to do Western-style fashion shoots, as well as photo shoots for posters and magazine advertisements. Both the advertising and media industries were growing in Japan at the time and were full of youthful energy. In her work, Kawakubo learned to use the power of images in order to create something with impact. Unsatisfied with the clothing available for use in the fashion shoots she was styling, Kawakubo began designing her own clothes, launching Comme des Garçons in 1969.

From the early on, Comme des Garçons fashions were distinctive and remarkable. Kawakubo's work revolutionized the Japanese fashion industry. Until 1988 the clothes were nearly all monochromatic, layers of black on black—a look that ignited a trend so pervasive that the legions of well-dressed women who swarmed around Omotesando wearing head-to-toe black came to be nicknamed *karasu* ("crows"). With their tightly cropped hair and pointy shoes, they appeared part of some sort of austere fashion cult. They cut a swath in the fabric of Tokyo's sartorial landscape, and rocked the entire fashion world when the crispness, lines, and entirely new silhouette of Kawakubo's styles made it abroad.

It was only after visits by foreign journalists and buyers from Browns in London and Maxfield in Los Angeles that it occurred to Kawakubo that she might be able to expand her business by showing in Europe—which up to then she had not aspired to. At her first show in Paris, in 1981, the befuddled Parisian press dubbed her first collection "Hiroshima Chic." Since then, Comme des Garçons has been characterized by its avant-garde design, and Kawakubo has been hailed among the fashion-world cognoscenti as the second coming of Coco Chanel, for the way she has presented a new vision of the contemporary woman and served as a role model for the fashion industry.

While European designers are burdened by a history of couture, tailoring, and clothes for specific occasions (collections just of party dresses, evening wear, day wear, or the idea of "the gown"), Japanese design suffers no such hindrance. Kawakubo's designs, and her process, are particularly free from restriction. Working with a stable of patternmakers, she communicates her designs to them without prohibitive concern for the conventional rules about structure, construction, fabric, and how to cut it. Unlike the work

of Yohji Yamamoto (whose background includes studying design in Paris, attending fashion school, and working in his mother's atelier), Kawakubo's work operates in a wholly different paradigm.

Her designs are bold and new, even in so basic a sense as how the clothing is made. She might use fabrics made from new production techniques, or she might use the very tulle that patternmakers use to formulate their initial designs. Layers of muslin joined together, with one or two threads loosely stitched to give it shape—with frayed edges—is a signature element of a Comme des Garçons dress. The forms, too, can be challenging and playful. A skirt may look like it's hanging from another skirt, or a sweater may be layered atop another sweater. When first confronted with a Comme des Garçons garment, it can be momentarily disorienting as to how to put it on. (Is this an arm or a neck hole? Is this a sash or a suspender?) The sophistication of this fashion deconstruction has garnered Kawakubo significant international respect. Alexander McQueen, the doyen of couture's vanguard, designed a dress in homage to "Madame Rei." To further stretch the fabric of fashion's possibilities, she has also collaborated with artists and creators in other fields of design, an esteemed crew that includes Seigen Ono, Merce Cunningham, Sarah Moon, Timothy Greenfield-Sanders, Future Systems, and Gilbert & George.

Beyond the garments, the label has led the way in pushing design and presentation, moving faster than the most cutting-edge Japanese consumer, showing new formats and shapes even before people realize they want them. The fragrance bottle that rests on its side. The shop that is a labyrinth. The ads that feature no clothes but, instead, an ostensibly random street scene, or a sequence of video frames of an older gentleman waking up and stretching in bed. The company has also opened a retail shop on London's Dover Street called Dover Street Market, retailing a vast international pool of prestigious designer brands.

Kawakubo characteristically avoids explaining her fashions to the press, and while she has asserted that she does not consider herself a specifically Japanese designer, her restless obsession with the new embodies the drive of her generation. It is this push to always be ahead of the game, create something never before seen, and always move forward that is the foundation of fashion in Tokyo. This is the essence of *style deficit disorder*.

Installation views of an exhibition intended for Comme des Garçons's employees. The blown-up reproductions include images from Comme des Garçons's magazine *Six*, a large-format, black-and-white periodical that ran for nine issues bi-annually from 1988–91. Other images include advertisements for the brand. ***Opposite, bottom left:*** An example of Kawakubo's fabled *karasu* clothing.

Opposite, above: The Comme des Garçons flagship store in Minami-Aoyama, designed in collaboration with the architectural firm Future Systems in 1998. *Opposite, below:* London's Dover Street Market is a department store of "beautiful chaos," as Kawakubo describes the unique architectural spaces built for each of the brands and boutiques she has selected. *This page, above:* Jan Comme des Garçons, a shop on Kotto-dori in Minami-Aoyama, featuring original clothing designed in collaboration with the brand and Belgian artist Jan de Cock. *Opposite, bottom:* Kobe's Comme des Garçons boutique.

Eau de Parfum
50 ml natural spray

Eau de Parfum

Eau de parfum, is the original Comme Des Garçons Parfum, launched in 1994. A perfume that works like a medicine and behaves like a drug.

Labdanum
Styrax
Cedarwood
Cardamom
Cinnamon
Black Pepper
Honey
Rose
Cloves
Nutmeg
Incense
Sandalwood

COMME des GARÇONS
parfums PARFUMS

Opposite, above: Perfume bottle and package designed in collaboration with Marc Atlan. With no flat base, the bottle rests on one side. ***This spread:*** Looks from Comme des Garçons' S/S 2007 collection.

KAWAII HARAJUKU

SDDH (Style Deficit Disorder: Harajuku), stands for obsessive shopping disorder.
—Patricia Field

KAWAI

HARAJUKU

REBELLION IS CUTE

The girly revolution begins

by Makoto Sekikawa

First published in 1989, the fashion magazine *CUTiE* rode the wave of Japan's punk- and new wave–inspired street fashion scenes; it was a true product of all that happened in the 1980s pop scene. Intended as a culture and lifestyle magazine targeted at girls, *CUTiE* was a spin-off of the youth-culture magazine *Takarajima,* which first went into print in 1975 and was the primary media outlet for what was happening in Japan's youth scene through the 1980s.

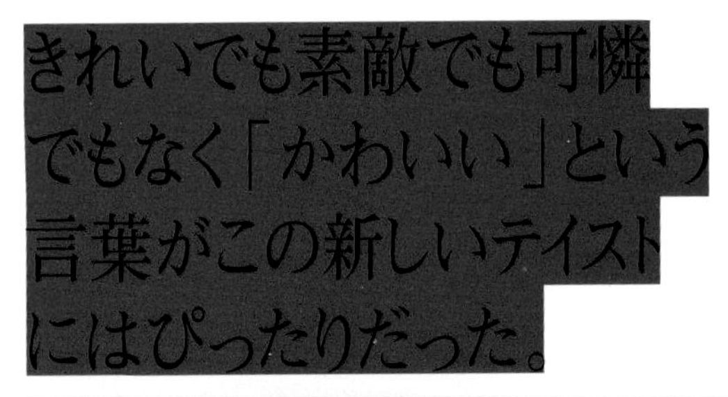

Takarajima was the first Japanese magazine to do features on the biggest names in the punk scene, like the Sex Pistols, The Clash, and The Damned. It also turned its attention to new wave, discussing the "new sound and concept" of groups such as Culture Club, XTC, and Frankie Goes to Hollywood. It showcased new fashion styles, like the latest designs by punk fashion progenitor Vivienne Westwood, and included regular features in each issue dedicated to Japan's own emerging punk and new wave trends. Young Japanese kids were spiking their hair into Mohawks with wax, wearing slim-fitting pants, and listening to this new music, all of which made them feel that they, too, could

Kawaii *came to be seen as the antithesis of traditional fashion geared toward an older generation of women, which emphasized womanliness and common sense.*

CUTiE icon Miwako Ichikawa in a mod, schoolgirl inspired feature from the June 1994 issue.

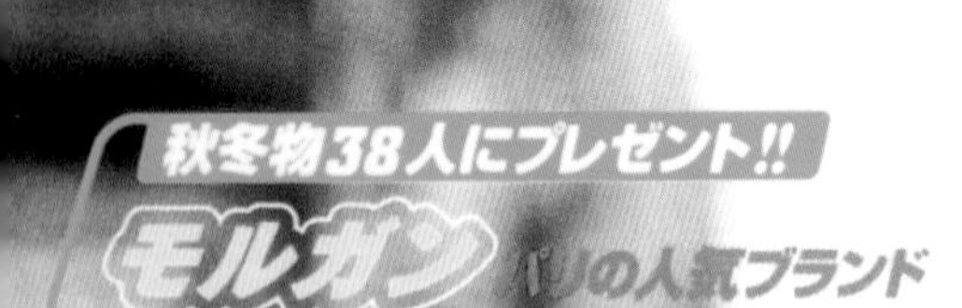

An October 1996 cover featuring the immensely popular model Hinano, with copy that reads "Retro style knits are *kawaii*." *Opposite top:* An editorial showing how to team biker jackets with sportswear from October 1995. *Bottom:* Miwako on the October 1994 cover.

Shortly after CUTiE's *launch, "street fashion" moved out of the margins of society and into the mainstream. This new trend flourished despite the economic recession that hit Japan in the 1990s. The new Heisei styles spread from Harajuku to all of Japan virtually overnight.*

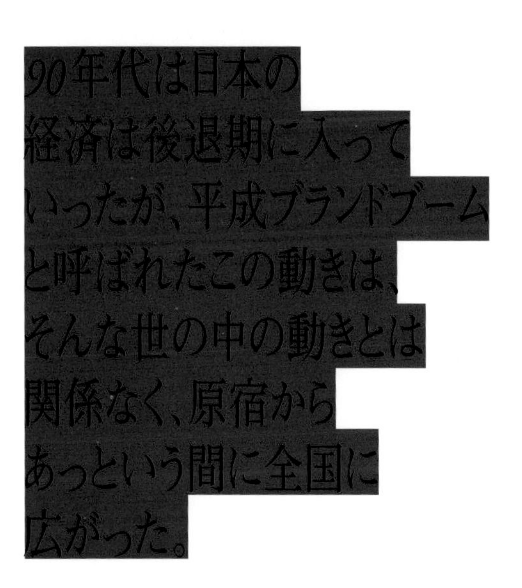

90年代は日本の
経済は後退期に入って
いったが、平成ブランドブーム
と呼ばれたこの動きは、
そんな世の中の動きとは
関係なく、原宿から
あっという間に全国に
広がった。

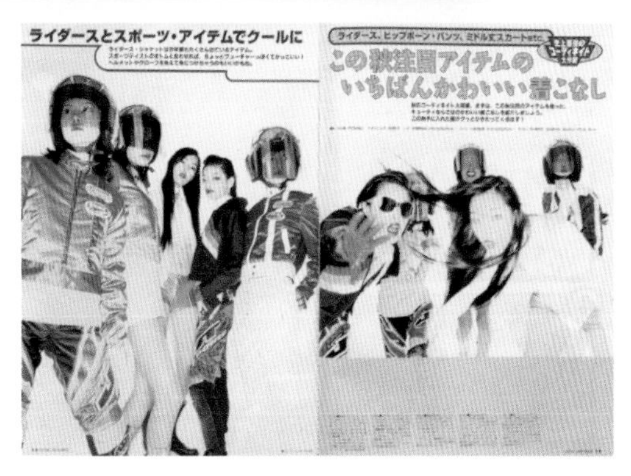

accomplish something new. Japanese kids started their own bands, made underground movies, formed theater groups, launched magazines, and made clothes. New wave groups emerging from Harajuku, such as the Plastics and YMO, quickly achieved international recognition, bringing the world's focus to the intense creative output emerging from the streets of Japan. It became impossible for *Takarajima* to keep up with it all. *CUTiE* was born.

During this same period in London, the magazine *i-D,* which featured fashion photos of kids on the street,

CUTiE welcomes in the new millenium with a special on what the coolest kids are wearing. The cool looking guy on the right is Hikaru, designer of Ura-Hara brand Bounty Hunter. ***Opposite top:*** An early Miwako cover wearing army surplus influenced style, October 1993. ***Opposite, bottom left:*** October 1995's catalogue style cover. ***Opposite, bottom right:*** "100 Kawaii Short Hair Styles."

was founded with the belief that a fashion magazine didn't have to be just a collection of photos of famous models wearing luxury-branded clothing. "There's something real [happening] in the street, and it's really creative"—this was *i-D*'s message, and it was also to be the message of *CUTiE*. Shortly after *CUTiE*'s launch, "street fashion" moved out of the margins of society and into the mainstream.

This new trend, which was called the Heisei Brand Boom ("Heisei" is a period of the Japanese calender beginning in 1989), flourished despite the economic recession that hit Japan in the 1990s. The new Heisei styles spread from Harajuku to all of Japan virtually overnight. By 2002, more conservative magazines such as *mc Sister* and *Olive* had gone out of print, and *CUTiE* was there to fill the void. Instead of reiterating the traditional messages that "sweet is best," and girls should be "well-behaved," "get married and become a good mother," *CUTiE* taught independence, "do whatever you want to do," and "do what you like."

It was *CUTiE* that first began using the word *kawaii*—a word that combines the concepts of "pretty" and "cute" in various ways—to identify what had long been a key component of Japanese aesthetics and apply it to fashion. *Kawaii* came to be seen as thc antithesis of traditional fashion geared toward an older generation of women, which emphasized womanliness and common sense. The styles featured in *CUTiE* were excessive, unbalanced or asymmetric, stagelike or humorous, and in extreme colors. The clothes were not necessarily practical; they were overly conspicuous, and not pleasing to the eye of most men. It was precisely this aspect, however, that was so appealing. There was rebelliousness in it. The tagline for *CUTiE* is: "For Independent Girls," a phrase that conveys the message, "Let's be stylish for ourselves—not to please men."

Harajuku street fashion had caught the world's attention. In May 2000, *CUTiE*'s publisher,

「新しい音、新しいコンセプト」のバンドが生み出した
ニューウェーブ、それらが極東の小さな国に伝わったとき、
その強烈な刺激とメッセージを受けた若者たちはまず
髪を切り、ワックスで立て、細身のパンツを穿いた。
自分たちもなにかできると勇気づけられていた。

Takarajima, staged fashion shows in New York and Hong Kong called *Tokyo Street 2000*. As editor-in-chief of the magazine, I would get endless questions from the press asking whether young Japanese women really liked these childish things. I used to answer, "The message is in the fact that they dare to wear these childish things." To be *kawaii* was to be daring and challenge the norm, a desire that runs rampant among Japanese youth.

Kawaii is a very important, distinctive feature of Japan's pop culture, seen in *anime* and comics and youth culture in general. What is generally true of youths all over the world is also true of young people in Japan, who strive for a counter-culture that resists established systems and values. Idealism mixed with rebelliousness and impatience, the culture of the Beatles, antiwar movements, student protests, the hippie movement, and punks—all these elements are in the same vein. It is about believing something's gone wrong in the world, about not trusting adults, about a drive to change the world with their own two hands. *Kawaii* is an expression of "No!" against the values imposed on the younger generation by the older, and it is a culture that was uniquely produced and developed by subtly sensitive young women in Japan.

Young Japanese kids were spiking their hair into Mohawks with wax, wearing slim-fitting pants, and listening to this new music, all of which made them feel that they, too, could accomplish something new.

Opposite: "Fall's Battle of the Coolest" is the October 2003 issue's main feature. *This page:* October 2004's cover girl was Chiaki Kuriyama of *Kill Bill* fame. The copy shouts "Rock for Fall. Go for Cool," with a star grammatically replacing the exclamation point in *CUTiE*-speak.

LAFORET SPRING

LAFORET
ラフォーレ

Harajuku's evolution from fashionable village to fashion capital is epitomized by the arrival of Laforet. In 1978, a part of the Tokyo Central Church was razed and replaced with a shopping mall. One might almost hear the angels singing when walking through the doors, were it not for the din blasting from the competing sound systems pumping music from every shop. At the time, Laforet was one of the tallest buildings in the area, dominating the landscape. The exterior gives scant evidence of the experience lying in wait. The sales, storewide and seasonal, are extraordinary—but shoppers must brace themselves for one of life's most intense shopping experiences. Everything—the music, the clothes, the riot of storefronts packed into its six floors (split into twelve half-floors), the shop girls screaming *irasshaimase* ("welcome!")—competes for attention. It is still a very Japanese experience. Shoppers swarm, but not aggressively. Somehow in all the madness no one gets killed. No stilettos in the neck. Every hair remains in place.

Laforet was built by real estate developer Mori Building, responsible for countless properties across Tokyo, including the Roppongi Hills shopping, residence, and museum complex. (*Mori* in Japanese means "forest," and for their fashion building they used the French translation.) Though there are fashion-dedicated buildings in other Tokyo neighborhoods, like Ikebukuro, Shinjuku, and Shibuya, and even some (such as Shibuya's Parco and Shibuya 109) that feature edgy fashion, Laforet was the first that would become solely devoted to youth culture. Brands like Hysteric Glamour and Ba-tsu opened their first shops in Laforet, and even now, after nearly thirty years, it remains the place for emerging fashion brands to break into the market, and the best reflection of what is happening on the streets.

Surprisingly, this wasn't always the case. Laforet was originally intended to cater more conventionally to shoppers drawn to established brands. But its first year in business was a flop. The original standard shop layout and staid design weren't drawing customers. Rethinking their approach, the management brought on Ryuki Matsumoto, the designer of the fashion brand Ba-tsu, to help attract customers and improve sales. His suggestions along with those of the participating shops culminated in a reworking of the interior. Long, deep stores were traded for a central stairwell and shallow shop space, giving shoppers a panoptical view. Young, emerging brands were encouraged to move in, reflecting Harajuku's new creative spirit. These changes became the foundation for the Laforet of today.

Beyond the layout, there were also early stumbles with image and branding. Laforet's first advertising campaign, designed by U.S.-based fashion illustrator Antonio Lopez—whose work was typically chic with European flair—didn't seem to click. Laforet continued to struggle to find its public image until art director Takuya Onuki was hired to create a series of ad campaigns in the mid-1990s. He had a preference for the use of nonliteral, quirky imagery. Rather than casting pretty women to present a precious sensibility in his ads, Onuki's graphics were more frequently humorous and a little trashy, with toy dogs modeling designer denim, or scenes of regular Americans going about daily life in their underwear. Along

Page 76: Art director Nagi Noda's floral version of King Kong with Fay Wray, a key visual for Laforet's spring 2005 promotion. **This spread:** Nude or Laforet. In 1997, Laforet's advertising campaign featured almost no clothing and used a bizarre choice of models. Designed by art director Onuki, the ads featured a busy boulevard sidewalk, a crowded airport terminal, a boardroom meeting, and a golf outing, and cast Western models. These images are so far removed from Harajuku's locality that it was a total assault to the senses. In the following year, the Nude or Laforet campaign continued but was recast using toy figures (**right**). This time, the scenes were of Americans at play, camping and skiing. **Below:** Underwear reappeared in this 2001 campaign.

with Onuki's designs, another art director, Nagi Noda, helped give Laforet its playful and distinctive image. The advertising campaigns she designed for Laforet blend a dreamlike fantasy with a playful stance.

Simultaneous with its role as launching pad for new cutting-edge designers, Laforet's success also marked the beginning of the commercialization of youth fashion culture in Japan. There was now a reliable and accessible market for smaller, breakaway labels, which inevitably led to some compromise in freedom and creativity. Laforet started teaming up with specific clothing brands and publishing companies of magazines (such as *An An* in the 1980s and *CUTiE* in the 1990s) to put on fashion shows in the building. Some of these designer brands wound up sucked into the hype machine, thinking they had finally hit the big time, only to be left flat when the media moved on to the next hot young designer. As with the rise of any subculture, there's nothing like success to bring out the followers, imitators, and wannabes. In the bright lights and attention, Mansion Makers were transformed into Designer Character brands, with all the commercial assimilation that the term implies. As a result, Laforet lost some of its steam in the late 1990s, when the newest cutting-edge designers sought alternatives to participating in the Laforet machine.

In 2006, Laforet made a comeback by creating a highly selective lineup of boutiques. It is as influential as ever, and the most diverse it's ever been. With its finger on the erratic pulse of Harajuku, it is a mish-mash of all the exotic tribes that make up Harajuku today, with floors dedicated to Goth-Loli fashion, edgy select shops, domestic old-time classics, and *gyaru* sexy styles that have spilled over from Shibuya 109, a newer shopping complex that opened in 2001 as Shibuya's answer to Harajuku's Laforet. To support a new generation of fashion talent, Laforet's management has even taken it upon itself to start a Laforet-operated shop called Side by Side as an incubating spot for young Japanese and international brands. In a neighborhood that is slowly being overrun by luxury businesses, Laforet is doing its part to keep fashion young, fresh, and fun.

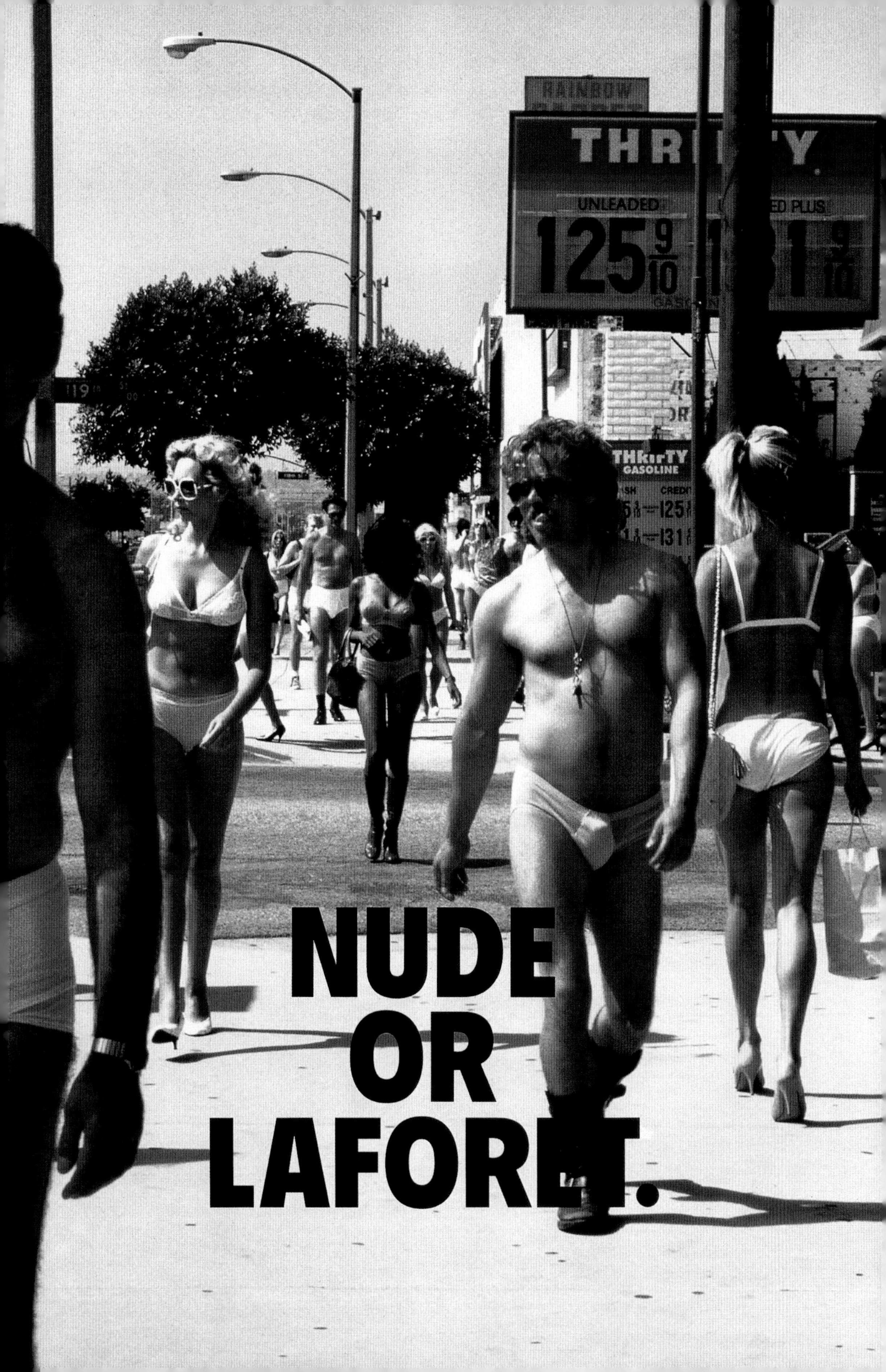
RAINBOW
UNLEADED
125 9/10
THRIFTY
GASOLINE
NUDE
OR
LAFORET.

Look!
Laforet

Advertising campaigns directed by Onuki for 1998 (*opposite*), winter 1995 (*above*), and 2001 (*right*).

This page (inset): Main images for 2003 autumn campaign designed by Noda.
This page (background): Stills from a television commercial airing for a 2004 Christmas campaign directed by Noda.
Opposite: The first advertising campaign Noda created for Laforet for the Christmas 2001 season.

MERRY X'mask. LAFORET.

Hysteric Glamou
MIAMI
Fuck
HYSTERIC

HYSTERIC GLAMOUR

ヒステリックグラマー

The chicksploitation image of Nobu Kitamura's Hysteric Glamour seems to have evolved from hazy stoner dreams of rock 'n' roll groupies. Imagine long-haired topless girls wearing hot pants and roller skates. But the twist that chief art director and designer Kitamura brings to his trashy Americana, B-movie chic is an unexpected, so-right spin on cute. From the time Kitamura opened his first shop in 1983 in Laforet, anyone *cool* shopped at Hysteric Glamour. The brand had attitude and power, and even if you didn't act rock 'n' roll, dressing in those clothes showed that you were part of the new spirit, the new youth movement.

After attending Tokyo Mode Gakuen, Kitamura started producing fashion shows and did design work for the brand Ozone Community. When he would later start Hysteric Glamour, Ozone Community was the backer, and the brand continues to be part of the Ozone Community group. Keeping an eye on the rapid changes in the fashion scene around him, and aware of the corporate takeover of Mansion Makers that turned them into Designer Character brands, Kitamura knew what he didn't want to create: a corporate business that produced safe, conservative clothing. He knew he wanted to design clothes that could only be made in Harajuku, by him, filtered through his particular sensibility. He loved American popular culture—lowbrow, white trash, rock, and porn culture—and saw real humor in it. He really loved that Americans didn't seem to take themselves so seriously. But rather than travel to America, he brought his version of America to Harajuku.

Hysteric Glamour was girly without being "girly" (no ruffles, please . . .). This was guitar-holding chicks sneering with their shiny, glossy lips. *CUTiE* got it and was on board from the beginning. The magazine regularly featured the brand and did fashion stories using Kitamura's clothing and aesthetic. The team involved in those shoots consisted of stylist Sonya Park, hair and makeup artist Katsuya Kamo, and photographer Takashi Homma. Internationally connected, equally aware of the art and high-fashion worlds, this team articulated a new Japanese fashion and photo subculture that was unlike anything that had come before—a multilayered reinvention of American trashiness that simultaneously incorporated Japaneseness, girliness, cuteness, and pop while keeping an edge. Hysteric Glamour advertisements, styled as centerfolds in *CUTiE,* might feature slim Japanese models who barely filled out their bikini tops, sporting pink glossy lips and clutching cute character handbags, hitchhiking at South Carolina truck stops. Here was Kitamura living out his teenage *Playboy* fantasies, through a fantasy and attitude that was irresistible to others as well.

Kitamura initially thought he wanted to become an artist, but his interest in fashion overtook that. He saw fashion's exciting creative potential and also enjoyed the sales and media aspects of the business, choosing to participate in the world of art as a patron and collaborator. He did this by becoming a publisher of photography books, starting in 1993, working with Japanese photographers he admires, such as Daido Moriyama, Nobuyoshi Araki, and Shoji Ueda, as well as Western photographers such as Terry Richardson, Cindy Sherman, Jack Pierson, and Dean Sameshima. This has meshed seamlessly with his innovative advertising for Hysteric Glamour, employing Richardson, painter Rita Ackerman, and B-movie king Russ Meyer as guest art directors on shoots.

" DAMN RIGHT. SHE'S DOING IT TO DEATH AGAIN ! "

THE
ORIGINAL MOTION PICTURE
STAYIN' BUSY PRODUCTIONS
PRESENTS

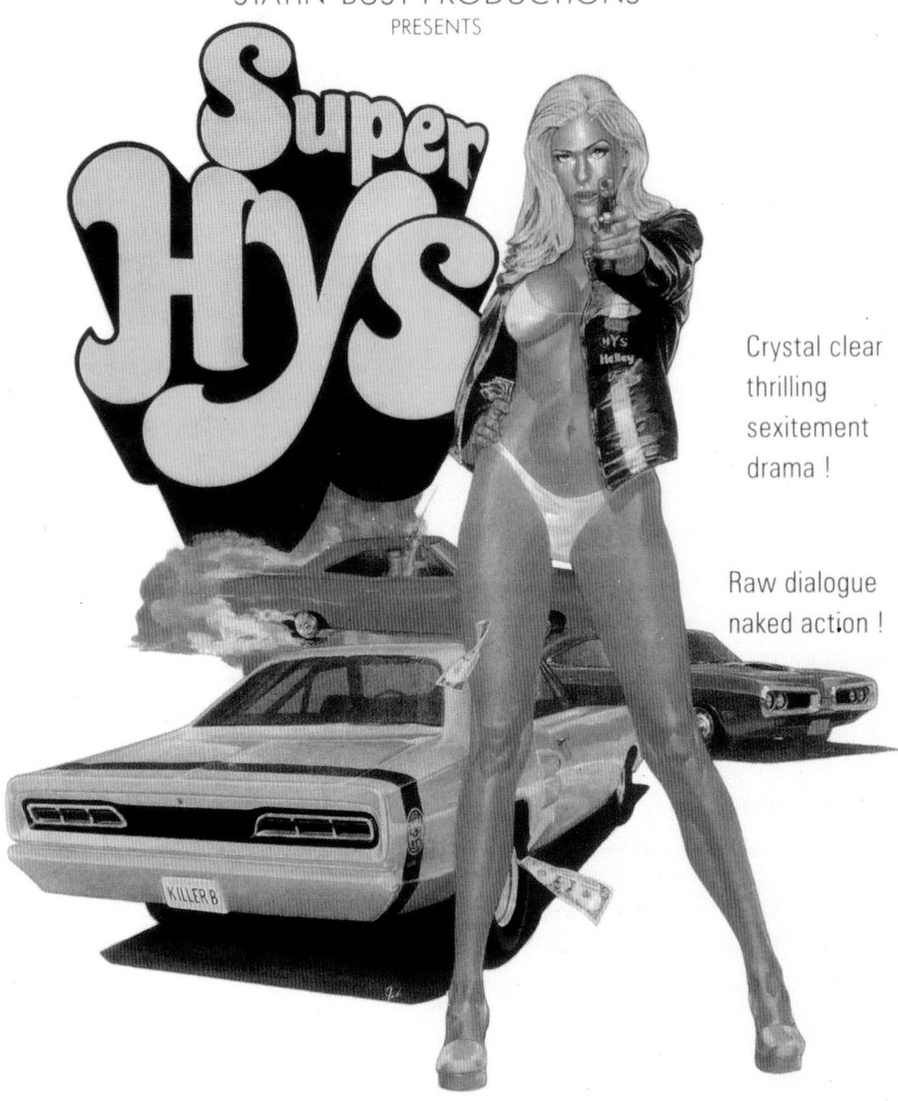

Starring
SUPER HYSTERIC. SUPER HEAVY. SUPER DOPE and KILLER B
Music by WONDER MIKE· Written by ALEX BABY· Produced and Directed by JAMES LEBON
TECHNICOLOUR PANAVISION From HYSTERICS A HYSTERIC GLAMOUR COMPANY
Original sound track available exclusively on HYSTERIC Records & Tapes

Page 84: A clear reference to Madonna's photography book *SEX* (in a bubblegum and cotton-panty version), this image was taken by the same team that helped establish the Hysteric Glamour advertising aesthetic: stylist Sonya Park, photographer Takashi Homma, and hair and makeup artist Katsuya Kamo. The model is Miwako, who, in representing an unconventionally "cute" sort of beauty, became the *CUTiE* icon. *This page:* A magazine advertisement styled after a movie poster. *Opposite:* An assortment of retro-styled stickers.

HYSTERIC LOVE MAKER
© 1999 HYSTERIC GLAMOUR
TEAM
HYSTERIC GLAMOUR
eXPERT
MADE
Miss Behave
© 1999 HYSTERIC GLAMOUR
GLAMOUR
© 2000 HYSTERIC GLAMOUR

Pages 88–89: "Fuck House Work!" The trash aesthetic of these Hysteric Glamour images used in displays, T-shirts, promotional items, and ads is comprised of chicksploitation images from 1970s America, rock concert posters, fast cars, and faster women. *Center:* "Joey Hysteric" is a new children's line launched in 2006. *Opposite:* This was part of a series of monthly centerfolds done for *CUTiE*, shot by Rowland Kirishima, as take-offs of *Playboy* centerfolds. It was a bit of an insider joke, with the reference lost to the general readership.

Hysteric
Glamour
Hysteric December Girl
Miwako
HYSTERIC GLA
TOKYO LONDON
Phone : 03-3478-8471

This page: Terry Richardson shot this 1999 ad campaign. It was one of the first campaigns that Hysteric Glamour ran in multiple magazines. *Opposite:* Kitamura has published many books of contemporary photography, including the work of Patti Smith (***top left***), Daido Moriyama (***top right***), and Terry Richardson (***bottom, all***).

TION
TH
Daido
hysteric
terryrichardson

A photo shoot for *CUTiE* by photographer Takashi Homma, Park's long-time collaborator.

SONYA PARK
ソニアパーク

Sonya Park is the fashion stylist most recognized as responsible for the West's sense of the current quirky, funky style coming out of Japan. She is *the* stylist the *kawaii* movement. Park's the one who put together mismatched patterns, fishnet stockings layered over purple tights under cut-off jeans with a dress on top, or a Louis Vuitton handbag paired with hair pinned up like a Mohawk. Cute, punky, funky. In the world of Japanese fashion, she's a legend—and she's not even Japanese!

Park was born in Korea and grew up in Hawaii. As a teenager, she couldn't relate to what was going on in American fashion during the 1980s: Calvin Klein, Brooke Shields, tight pants, no underwear, sexy, sexy, sexy. Her father, who had lived in Korea during the Japanese occupation, spoke Japanese. He would often take her to the local Japanese supermarket, where she would buy Japanese fashion magazines such as *An An* and *Ryuko-Tsushin*. In these magazines she first saw Comme des Garçons clothes, and she became convinced that the most exciting trends in fashion and avant-garde design were coming from Tokyo, not America or Europe.

In 1987, in her late teens, despite having no background in fashion, she packed up and moved to Tokyo, where she imagined the streets would be swarming with people dressed in Comme des Garçons—but the reality was disappointing. Japan was still entering the international market, and Tokyo seemed provincial, grasping, and tacky rather than refined and fashionably avant-garde. However, Park stayed, landing a job as an assistant stylist at the trendy magazine *Gap*. Soon thereafter, she had an opportunity to do some styling for *CUTiE*: six to eight pages of "something interesting," such as mixing vintage, high-end fashion with streetwear, on a shoestring budget but without restrictions. This was the start of a long and illustrious relationship with the magazine.

The *CUTiE* spreads (and *CUTiE* in general, for that matter) weren't much respected by the mainstream Japanese fashion industry, who considered them child's play. As she continued styling spreads for the magazine, Park was able to borrow clothes for the shoots from hot new Heisei brands such as Hysteric Glamour and As Known As. These were designers who had grown up thinking of fashion as part of pop culture and who aimed their designs at the young kids. Park mixed the Heisei brand fashions with elements of vintage or high fashion, combinations that sparked an entirely new aesthetic. The kids lapped up her look. Park and her crew (hair and makeup artist Katsuya Kamo and photographers Kazunari Tajima and Takashi Homma) had been influenced by Western magazines such as *The Face* and *i-D,* but had captured the new creative remix reality of the Japanese street fashion scene, creating their own new style. Their work struck a nerve, turning *CUTiE* into the most important subculture magazine in Japan.

At the peak of its popularity, from 1995 to 1999, *CUTiE*'s circulation surged to 600,000 with twice-monthly distribution. *CUTiE* finally started to receive the recognition it was due, and suddenly everyone wanted to be a part of it. Designer Junya Watanabe, who has his own label under the Comme des Garçons umbrella, loaned his clothes to Park for a shoot and soon sold out every design that had been included. Editors from the fashion capitals of London and Paris would see Park's design portfolio, comment on its originality, and then find ways to copy her look. Park began to get fan letters from girls excited that she and her crew were not only representing what girls were wearing in Harajuku, but adding to it and introducing new ideas.

Not everyone was so appreciative. Many claimed that *CUTiE* was meant for the *busu-kawaii* (meaning "ugly cute") girls. *CUTiE*'s tagline, "For Independent Girls," was mocked and often misquoted as "for lonely girls who couldn't get dates." But for Park and the girls *CUTiE* spoke to, fashion was about breaking from convention, not attracting men. These were the girls who would come to Harajuku dressed so outrageously and inventively that they were photographed by passersby. They had put into practice what Park wanted: she wanted people not to copy the looks shown in the magazine's pages, but to be inspired to create their own images.

This page: Examples of Park's work for *CUTiE* dating from 1994–1997. *Opposite:* Photography by Takashi Homma. Park and Homma collaborated for many years on numerous shoots. Homma's interest was in documenting youth culture, not making fashion pictures per se. Park was trying to create an impact as strong as Comme des Garçons without using their clothes.

Everyday I Love Fake Fur

毎日着れるフェイクファー

フワフワであったかいフェイクファー。冬にしか使えないから、冬の
そこで、毎日着れてキラリと光るフェイクファーの着こなしに挑戦。
地味ハデなバランスが、毎日フェイクファーを楽しみたいキューティ

photography Yoshie Tomi
パラドック
が渋谷にオ
京都を拠点に展開して
ックス』が、初の直営店
した。
ちょっとパンクっぽい
ウエアが多く、チェック
の7〜8分丈パンツや、
です。
カットワークが面白い
もオススメ。11月にオー
ラドックス東京』行って
パラドックス東京ショ
谷区渋谷2・3・3 青
・5485・6365
無休
photograph

Spreads from *CUTiE* dating 1994–1997. ***This page:*** Hysteric Glamour advertorial images for *CUTiE* with photography by Takashi Homma.

POPEYE & OLIVE

ポパイ アンド オリーブ

First published in 1978, *Popeye* (think "pop" and "eye") focused on new music, new culture, and a new sense of style distinct from the more staid men's magazines that had come before. With the tagline, "The Magazine for City Boys," early issues focused on casual urban American fashions, particularly those associated with California's recreational lifestyle culture of outdoor wear, college gear, and sports and sportswear from the skateboard and surf scenes. *Popeye*'s version of culture was a big hit, and drew a sharp line between itself and those who were into the burgeoning punk and new wave scenes. By the early 1980s, *Popeye* had evolved into one of the biggest mainstream men's fashion magazines in Japan. *Olive,* launched in 1982 as a girls' version of *Popeye,* featured Japanese models (including photos of its readers) until about 1985, when it found its signature image—natural, soft, and mature—and changed its tagline to "The Magazine for Romantic Girls." Featuring imported brands like agnès b. and Margaret Howell worn by foreign models in new trendy neighborhoods like Daikanyama and Hiroo, the magazine represented a slightly adult fantasy image that young Japanese girls could aspire to. Popular through the 1980s, after which it was eclipsed by *CUTiE, Olive* folded in 2002.

Opposite: In 1977 punk became a worldwide phenomenon. Meanwhile, *Popeye* readers were reading about Italian casual wear in this December 1977 issue. *This page, clockwise from top: Olive* provides a sense of the exoticism in their covers, as in these March 1985 and December 1984 issues. *Popeye*'s October 2002 and July 1994 issues keep with their core focus on street fashion.

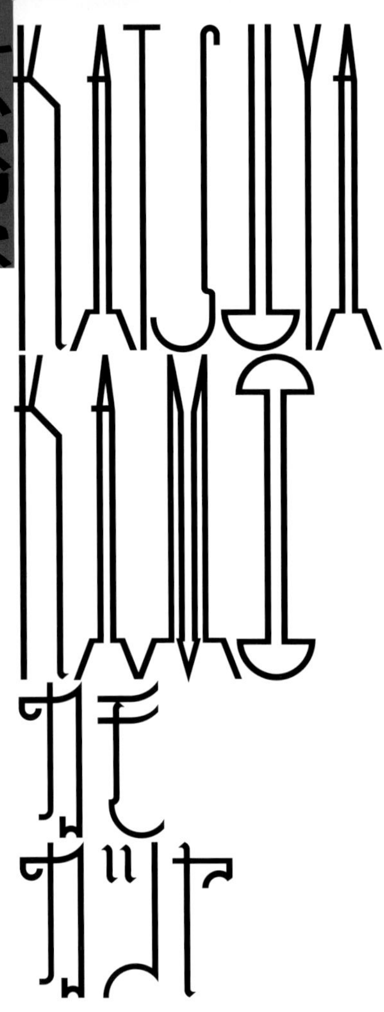

Since 1995, hair and makeup artist Katsuya Kamo has worked with Japanese brands such as Comme des Garçons, Junya Watanabe Comme des Garçons, and UNDER COVER, as well as Belgian designer Haider Ackerman's label. Where Japanese street fashion went to extremes of design, Kamo kept pace, incorporating a range of materials in his hairstyles that knew no bounds. While his styling in a runway context allowed for otherwise impractical hairstyles, his hair for editorials was no less extreme. In his hands hair became an object that, at times, enveloped the model. Designers chose to work with him because of what he brought to the table and contributed to the whole look. The homogeneity of naturally straight, jet-black Japanese hair helped to dramatically underscore his adventurous invention, and in fact Japanese girls and boys are fairly adventurous when it comes to hair styles, cuts, color, and accessories, recognizing that individuality can really shine in a realm where everyone is so similar. Kamo's work presented an idea of glamour decidedly far removed from chichés, and his sense of beauty—his interest in combining cute, punk, sexy—was decidedly Japanese in feel.

Photographs from *Libération Style* (2004) by the celebrated Japanese photographer Hiromix; styling by Aya Tanizaki; all hair and makeup by Kamo.

This page, inset: Kamo's notebooks, used in preparation for runway shows. The Polaroids are of mannequins and the synthetic hair used to create hair sculptures. The top notebook is for Junya Watanabe Comme des Garçons' 1997 collection, with hair inspired by *Edward Scissorhands*. ***Opposite:*** A look created for the magazine *Purple Fashion*. Kamo also incorporates unorthodox materials into these constructions. These silhouettes help turn the runway and fashion pages into pure fantasy or drama.

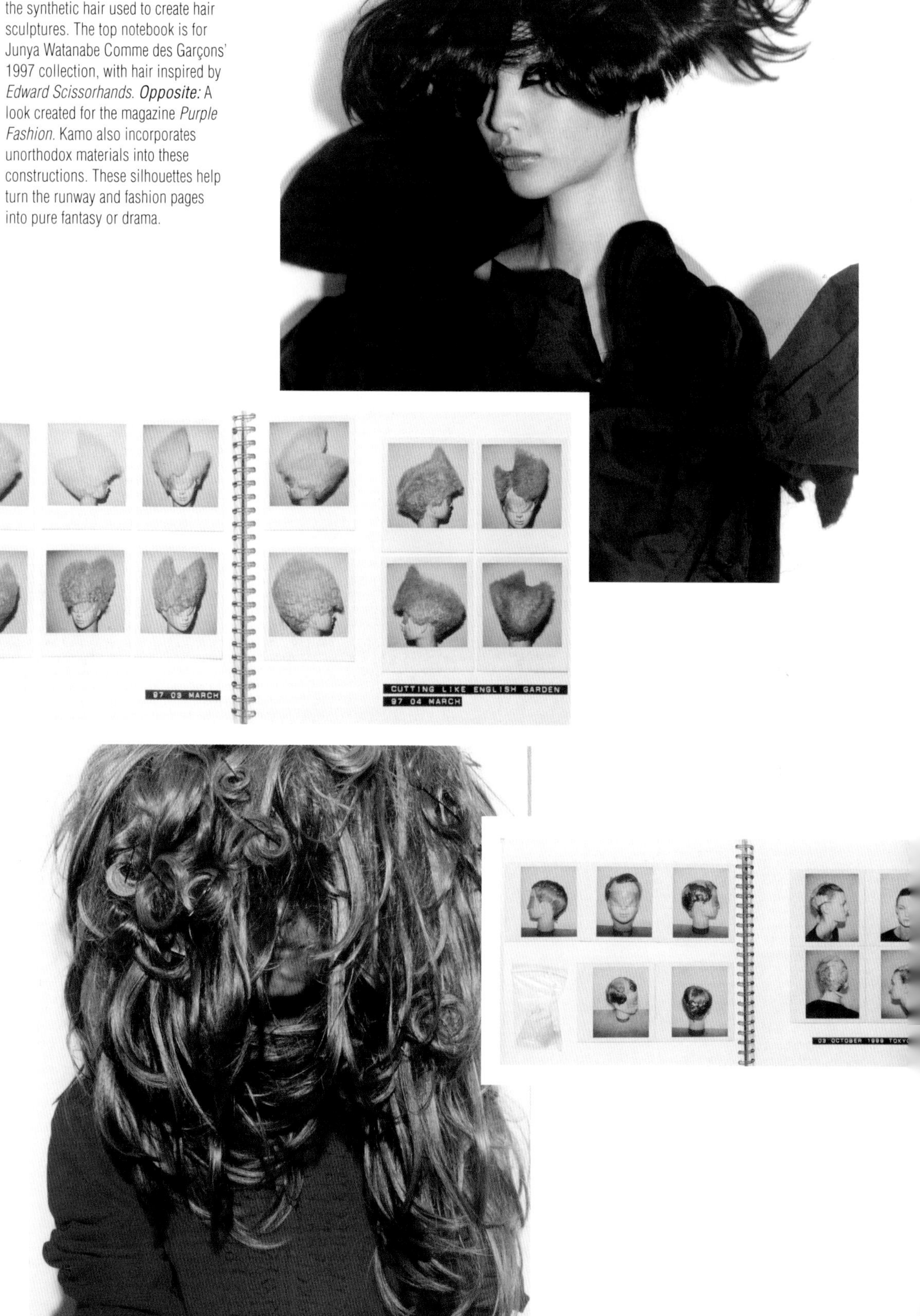

スーパーラヴァーズ

SUPER LOVERS

スーパーラヴァーズ

An iconic clubwear brand, Super Lovers was launched into international popularity in the 1990s after a club kid was photographed wearing the brand's clothing head-to-toe at a 1989 London rave called "Summer of Love 2." When the picture ran in *The Face,* it made the brand a cult hit. The following year, Super Lovers presented its first collection in London. DJ Towa Tei, who was famous on the New York club scene, was also known for wearing Super Lovers' T-shirts. Both the characters and the logo had a distinct Japanese sensibility, tapping into an international fascination with Japanese pop culture and Tokyo's club scene. Once the brand had achieved recognition in the West, it found domestic allure as well. Coming at a time of flagging interest in the DC brands, Super Lovers' club energy made its fashions seem fresh and exciting, and its acid-happy characters helped brighten a period of economic woe. Super Lovers was known for organizing club parties at venues all over Japan, including such famous spots as Shibaura Gold, near Tokyo Bay. The brand drew strength from its close association with music trends and promoted itself through these club events and outfitting DJs with Super Lovers gear. With the fade-out of techno, the volume of the brand faded out a bit as well.

Left: An advertising image in *FRUiTS* magazine for the Lover's Rock line. *Right:* Promotional materials for the Super Lovers and Lover's Rock brands. The panda characters "Ken" and "Merry" were created for an event at Tokyo-area club Shibaura Gold, and would go on to appear on Super Lovers' T-shirts, clothing, and bags. The Super Lovers logo is the pink heart in the diamond.

A HOUSE OF CREATIVE CULTURE
WORK FOR SUPER LOVERS co.,ltd.
LOVER'S ROCK
SUPER LOVERS
NEW WAVE
PRODUCED BY YASUHARU TANAKA

SUMMER OF LOVE 2000
SUPER LOVERS
LOVE IS THE MESSAGE
2000.5.20(sat)
START

15000円以上お買い上げの方に SUPER LOVERS staff only not for sale AMBRELLA PRESENT!
www.superlovers.co.jp

CYBER & BEYOND HARAJUK

&

CYBER & BEYO

FRUiTS
50
LOTTERIA
ロッテリア
原

In the ebb and flow of Tokyo street fashion, the late 1980s and early 1990s seemed to float by in a creative lull. The rise to mainstream acceptance of what had been a cutting-edge street fashion scene brought with it a willingness by some (perhaps too many) to accept now-established brands and styles as a ready-made entrée to "cool." However, photographer Shoichi Aoki saw signs of life—where else?—on the streets of Harajuku. Noticing that the kids there were taking a less passive approach, recombining unexpected elements and using fashion as personal statement—even street art—he launched the magazine *FRUiTS* in 1997. Aoki wanted to document and fuel what he saw as a movement and an inspiration. As the magazine's creator and primary photographer, he would hang out in Harajuku sometimes four days a week, taking pictures and talking to the coolest-looking kids he could find. "I wanted to photograph only the most stylish people," he said. "I wasn't interested in lower-level fashion kids." Only wearing an outfit like no one else earned you the attention of his lens.

So the kids started upping the ante, wearing stuff that no one else would wear in order to be photographed by Aoki. The short Q-and-A texts that accompanied the photographs called attention to the fact that the kids who made it into the magazine were assembling their looks from multiple shops and designers. The questions asked the kids for their "point of fashion" and "current obsession," further emphasizing the personal, improvisational, whimsical nature of what was going on. Trends started. There was a new movement virtually every three months. Everyone was trying to outdo everyone else. Wanting something unique, they might still buy Heisei or DC brand items, but they'd rip them up or layer them, altering the effect. Everyone became a customizer, essentially making their own brands.

To be photographed by Aoki meant that you were a fashion god, and because you got into *FRUiTS* by your own creative inspiration, the kids pushed themselves off Olympian heights of fashion excess. "What's the world record for the number of different patterns you could possibly wear at once? How many badges can you attach to your leather jacket?"

On Sundays the main streets of the neighborhood (including Omotesando) were closed to traffic, creating a "Pedestrian Paradise" (Hokoten) that amounted to a freeform outdoor fashion catwalk and streetside mall where clothes and accessories were bought and sold. Kids would perch outside Laforet or promenade along Omotesando (where even today photo crews from Japanese fashion magazines position themselves, waiting for the future to walk by), hoping they'd make the grade.

Guys were starting to dress up as much as girls were, and though *FRUiTS* featured photographs of both, Aoki decided to launch a new magazine in 2005, called *TUNE,* to capture what the boys were up to. ("Usually developing your sense of style is through trial and error," Aoki said, "but these boys somehow got it right from the beginning.")

Just like bands, some of the kids were one-hit wonders and some were stars, appearing in the pages of *FRUiTS* or *TUNE* again and again. Hot streaks could last for about a year, but the magazine was always waiting for the next kid to land from planet What-

Are-You-Wearing? While the scene around the magazines definitely drove the kids to new creative heights and some brilliant innovations, there was ultimately not much in the way of deeper significance to much of these fashion hijinks. Many (but certainly not all) of the styles lacked the social import associated with movements like punk or hip-hop.

In 1999, the party essentially ended when the Hokoten was reopened to motor traffic on Sundays. Though there are certainly still kids dressed to their teeth and strolling Omotesando ready for their close-ups, and *FRUiTS* and *TUNE* are both still in publication, it's both a measure of the fickleness of fashion trends that Harajuku youths are no longer sporting such colorful plumage en masse, and a testament to the creativity of those that remain.

Images from *FRUiTS*, spreads covering 1997 to 2007.

TUNE

7 2006
No.21
チューン
650yen

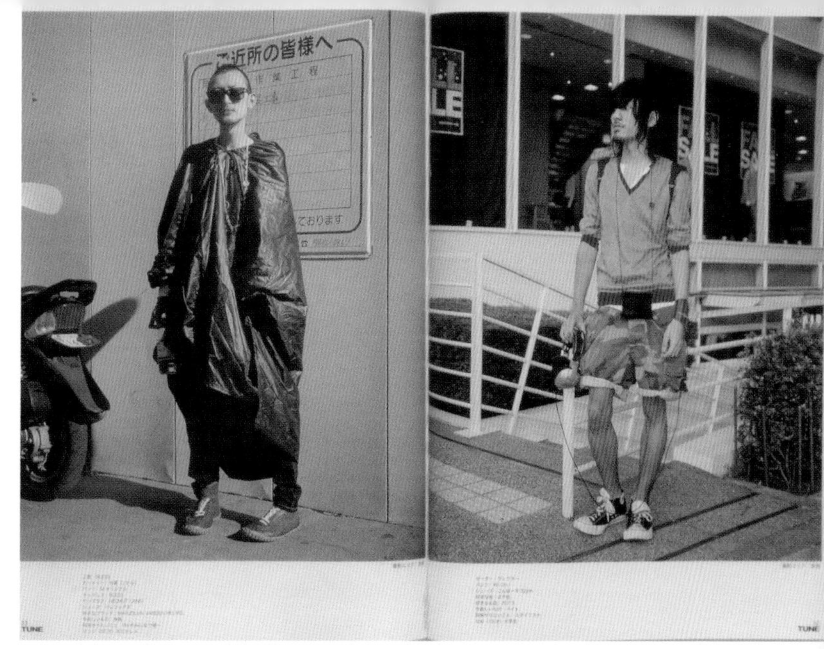

Images from *TUNE*, spreads covering 2004 to 2007.

Fötus

Cyber fashion. The Tokyo version of the trance, the cyberpunk look walked the Hokoten Harajuku runway cute as *anime* cupcakes, with the spacey gear made famous on the pages of the early issues of *FRUiTS*. Fötus was originally started by designer Masahiro Saito in 1997, just as the visual-kei band scene was taking shape. Like Belgian designer Walter Van Beirendonck and his label W.&L.T. (which was hugely popular in the mid-1990s, particularly in Japan), Fötus drew inspiration from space exploration and technology, adding a touch of Goth with the metallic and neon color schemes. Fötus's rubber, nylon, synthetic fur, and hologram prints were the perfect costumes for the theatrical stage performances by the band GLAY (and its female fans) and trance DJs alike. The brand's logo, a fetus with a dangling umbilical cord, represented the birth of something new, as surely no other designer had dared or thought to make neon kimonos. Though the brand is not as visible as it was in its heyday, it can still be seen in the pages of *KERA* magazine.

"The Future is Bright" is the slogan of Masahiro Saito's brand Fötus. His emphasis is on creating clothing that challenges the wearer to stand out. The brand and its bright colors and artificial materials were the outfit of choice for millenial club kids. Saito views techno music festivals as places that unite young future-minded people who can change the world in a positive way.

20471120

Since 1994, 20471120 (representing November 20, 2047) has been responsible for outfitting Harajuku-ites in what looked, at first glance, like extraterrestrial costumes. Masahiro Nakagawa's background as an artist, paired with Lika Azechi's love of British tailoring, yielded a penchant for fantasy and otherworldliness. This duo became notorious in part for treating fashion as spectacle and entertainment along with a vision of the future, as the brand name implies. Tra I Venti (a nickname adopted after some difficulties with Japanese trademark bylaws) used digital hardcore as a soundtrack for their shows. Their 1995 debut Tokyo collection, "Ultra," was open to a general admission audience at a cost of 2,500 yen per ticket. A thousand eager fans were treated to a show featuring models cast from the Kinoshita circus and clothing that seemed to take inspiration from astronauts and insects: playful, bizarre, risky, and refreshing. Fashion students saw this as a newly granted license to be just as original, experimental, and playful. The brand flourished, taking its antics to Paris numerous times starting in 1998. Artist and impresario Takashi Murakami included the brand in his famous *Superflat* exhibition in 2001. Its popularity and creative output peaked that same year, just as new brands like Uniqlo were coming to the fore with their low-priced, mass-produced fashions. In reaction, Nakagawa launched (also in 2001) the Recycle Project, a custom-remake couture brand that has even set up a temporary atelier in the Smithsonian.

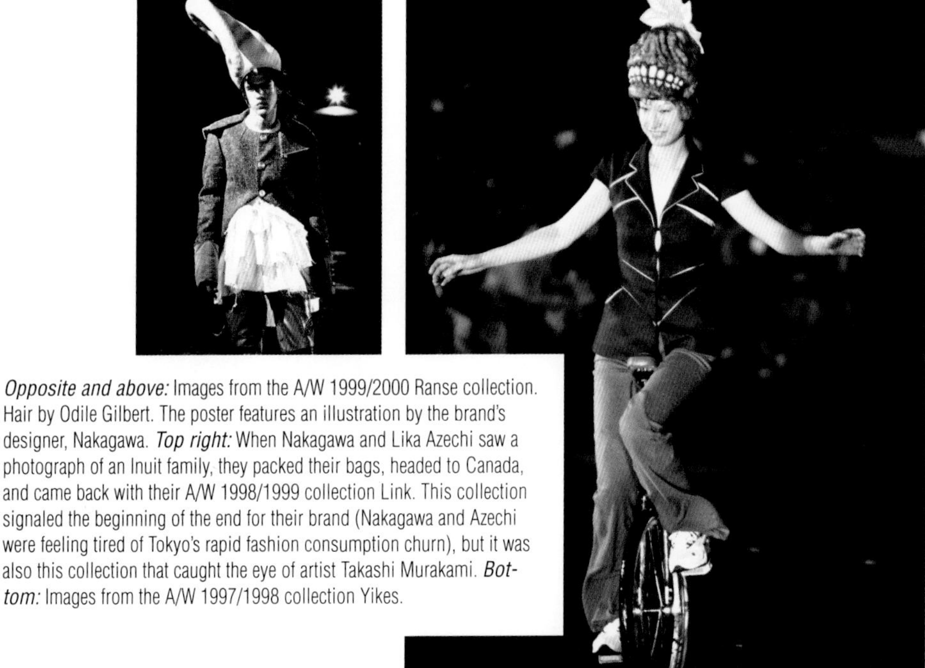

Opposite and above: Images from the A/W 1999/2000 Ranse collection. Hair by Odile Gilbert. The poster features an illustration by the brand's designer, Nakagawa. *Top right:* When Nakagawa and Lika Azechi saw a photograph of an Inuit family, they packed their bags, headed to Canada, and came back with their A/W 1998/1999 collection Link. This collection signaled the beginning of the end for their brand (Nakagawa and Azechi were feeling tired of Tokyo's rapid fashion consumption churn), but it was also this collection that caught the eye of artist Takashi Murakami. *Bottom:* Images from the A/W 1997/1998 collection Yikes.

Masaki Matsushima

マサキマツシマ

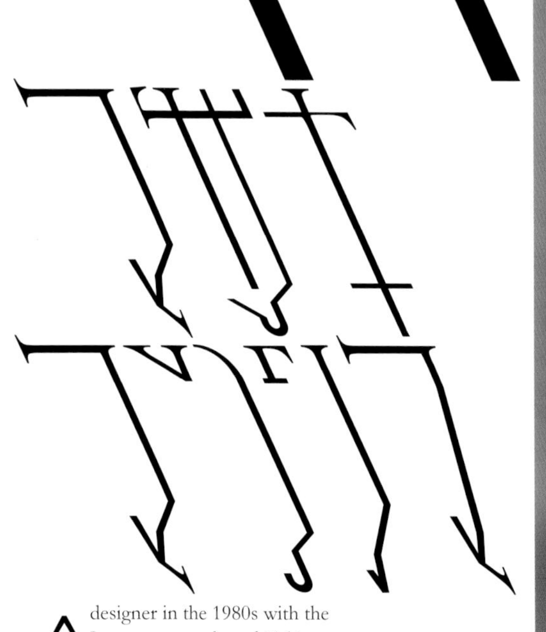

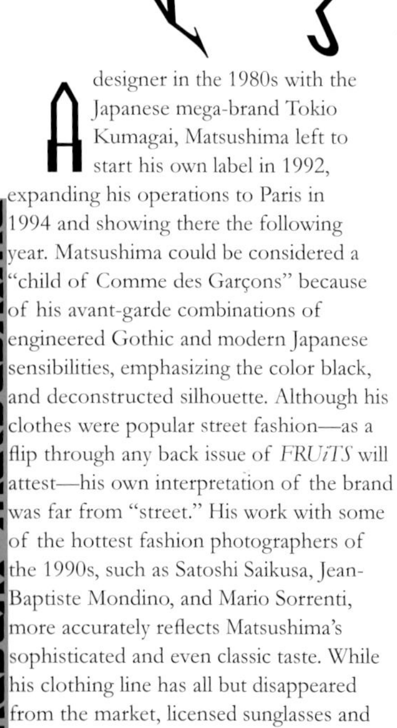

A designer in the 1980s with the Japanese mega-brand Tokio Kumagai, Matsushima left to start his own label in 1992, expanding his operations to Paris in 1994 and showing there the following year. Matsushima could be considered a "child of Comme des Garçons" because of his avant-garde combinations of engineered Gothic and modern Japanese sensibilities, emphasizing the color black, and deconstructed silhouette. Although his clothes were popular street fashion—as a flip through any back issue of *FRUiTS* will attest—his own interpretation of the brand was far from "street." His work with some of the hottest fashion photographers of the 1990s, such as Satoshi Saikusa, Jean-Baptiste Mondino, and Mario Sorrenti, more accurately reflects Matsushima's sophisticated and even classic taste. While his clothing line has all but disappeared from the market, licensed sunglasses and perfumes continue to represent the brand.

Opposite, top and bottom: Images from the S/S 1995 collection catalogue by photographer Satoshi Saikusa and stylist Mika Mizutani. *Opposite, left:* F/W 1995 advertising visual by Jean-Baptiste Mondino, with hair and makeup by Topolino. *This page:* S/S 1992 debut collection catalogue photograph by Saikusa and Mizutani.

BEAUTY : BEAST

ビューティービースト

In 1991, Takao Yamashita started beauty : beast just as Tokyo's most edgy were starting to tap into the deconstructed taste of the grunge scene and emerging Belgian fashion brands such as Ann Demeulemeester and Martin Margiela (both influenced by Japanese fashion). The Nagasaki-born designer's taste combined Gothic and conceptual elements, as the name would suggest, and attracted adherents in both the fashion and music world. His sights were set on high fashion runways, showing first in Osaka, then switching in 1994 to Paris. He continued to produce his clothes in Europe even when he moved his presentations back to Tokyo for the 1995–1996 autumn/winter collection. By 1998, the brand enjoyed domestic mainstream success with the youth market, even making license deals with major backers for a second line, 2 beauty : beast. Yamashita took a hiatus in 2000 with stints as a DJ and illustrator. The company currently boasts a beauty salon spin-off, Cosmatrix; a record label, Neven; and a U.K.–based online shop, Oki-ni.com.

The structured qualities of beauty : beast's clothing hints at designer Takao Yamashita's background in architecture; his conceptual adaptation of Biblical verses from Ezekiel ("And you will know my name is the Lord; when you know my beast within thee..."), verses also adapted by Samuel L. Jackson's character in *Pulp Fiction*, hint at the brand's arch aesthetic sensibility.

Christopher Nemeth

クリストファー ネメス

A Tokyo-based British designer, Christopher Nemeth is one of fashion design's most underappreciated talents, as well as one of the most copied, as he has busily created original, technically complex unisex clothing for more than twenty-five years. Originally a painter, Nemeth had no formal fashion training before he formed a design collective called The House of Beauty & Culture in London in the early 1980s with Judy Blame and John Moore. The clothes were magpie, handmade-looking, three-dimensional constructions regularly featured in the pages of *i-D* magazine. In 1993 Nemeth was invited to Tokyo to participate in Hanae Mori's London Goes to Tokyo fashion show, along with Judy Blame, Leigh Bowery, and others. And he just never left. From his fashions outfitting the *FRUiTS* kids of the 1990s to those of the Harajuku kids today, Nemeth's clothes haven't changed much, nor do they need to; the overstitched denim, tweed, and cotton suits are oddly timeless.

Visuals circa 1987, when the designer moved to Tokyo permanently. ***Opposite and top:*** From *i-D* magazine's "The Conservative Issue" no. 37 June 1986, photographed by Mark Lebon. ***Bottom, left and right:*** Nemeth modeling his own recycled gear, photographed by Mike Owen. ***Center:*** the brand's Celtic inspired logo, designed and painted by Nemeth, which also appears painted within his Harajuku boutique.

TOKYO
HAIR
PHOTOGRAPHY BY
MASAYUKI
YOSHINAGA

GOTH-LOLI HARAJUK
GOTH-LOL

HARAJUKU

GOTHIC, LOLITA, VISUAL-KEI

First Kansai then the World (via Harajuku)

by Mariko Suzuki

As can be seen in America, where the difference between the East and West Coasts is reflected in the fashions of New York and Los Angeles, Japan also has a marked difference between east and west. Osaka, in Japan's west, has traditionally held a predilection for strength and individuality of style, whereas Tokyo, in Japan's east, leans more toward sophistication. Long, long ago, during the Edo period (1603–1867), the expression *iki* was used to describe stylish and cool things. In Osaka, someone *iki* wore brashly patterned kimonos that caught the eye. Tokyoites, however, looked down on these showy effects. For them, a palette of plain-colored outer layers, with only glimpses of a more elaborate inner lining, was considered stylish. Of course, that was a time when everyone in Japan wore kimonos.

These days most Japanese don Western clothing. This is only one of the numerous changes to Japanese culture since the Meiji era (1868–1912), when Japan first opened its doors to Western influences. In the sixty years since the end of World War II, Japanese designers have consistently copied Western-style clothing, leading to what has developed into an original Japanese look. However, historic regional differences of opinion about fashion that predate the Meiji era continue.

Interestingly, the more famous of these Western-style Japanese clothing designers have hailed from the Osaka region. Osaka, with its penchant for a powerful and

These Kansai creative types made clothes that were definitely unusual and challenged conventional thinking—"Where would I even wear this? Is this for everyday, or for the stage?"

conspicuous style, nurtures creativity. The now well-known Gothic and Lolita (Goth-Loli) style began in the creative environment around Osaka (i.e., Osaka and Kobe). Hereafter, I shall follow custom in Japan and refer to these Osaka regional designers collectively as Kansai designers. These Kansai creative types made clothes that were definitely unusual and challenged conventional thinking—"Where would I even wear this? Is this for everyday, or for the stage?"

Famous early Kansai designers include Kazuko Ogawa, Marble/Visible (known for Goth-Loli clothing with a modernized take on Victorian-era princess sleeves), and alice auaa (known for their signature ripped-gauze clothing—probably more Gothic-inspired than Goth-Loli). Later, in 1999, Victorian maiden attracted notoriety for their twenty casket-shaped "beds." Each of these Gothic-style brands was born in Kansai.

oon, flamboyant Osaka-based bands, though all male, began to wear what were intended as the women's version of the Goth-Loli style. This *visual-kei* (meaning "Japanese visual music style") placed great importance on the gorgeous spectacle created onstage, a performance with some similarity to traditional Kabuki, where all the roles—both male and female—are played by men. The fans copied, wearing these romantic yet classic designs out and about, on the streets.

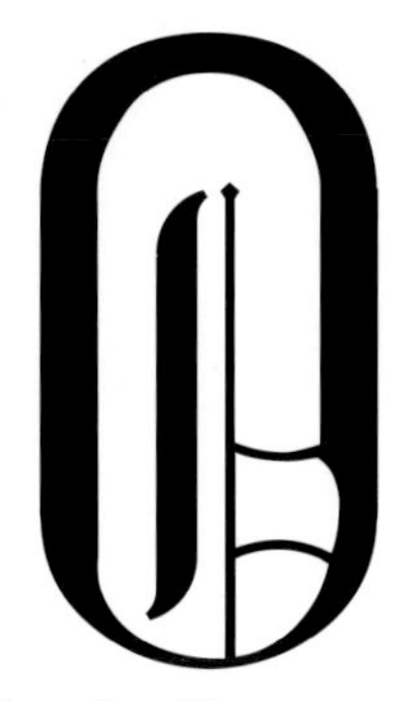ne popular band, Malice Mizer, inspired many such young female fans. The original lead musician, Mana (guitar and synthesizer), wore Goth-Loli clothing by Kazuko Ogawa and appeared frequently in magazines and on television. Not only did fans copy his clothes, they mimicked his every word and gesture, adopting his air of gentility. Mana was the Goth-Loli fashion world's leader. In late 1995, the band added the lithe, tall, fine-featured singer Gackt, who became a heartthrob for girls and boys alike and launched the band to national fame—helping to bring Goth-Loli to all of Japan.

By 1997 the first signs of a Gothic trend in America began to infiltrate Japan. Marilyn Manson's *Antichrist Superstar* became a hit, and Manson toured in Japan for the first time. In 1998, Madonna released her single "Frozen," and in the video (directed by the visionary Chris Cunningham) she donned dark Gothic clothing before transforming into a flock of black crows. Meanwhile, in Europe, Jean Paul Gaultier was announcing his new Gothic line of clothing. But Japan's Gothic fashion was clearly different.

In the West, bondage was a central theme to the Gothic style, and sexy clothes were dominant. Japan's Gothic style tended to the opposite. Abstinence, girlishness, and virginity were prominent themes. Girls covered up so very little skin was left exposed, and wore lace and other frilly material almost to excess. They covered their legs with knee-high socks

関西方面のクリエイター達は、「こんなのどこに着るの？」「これ舞台用の服なの？」と思うような、「フツーじゃない服」を作るパワーがあるのです。

and wore Odeko shoes, characterized by a prominent rounded toe, rather than high heels. It has been suggested that this style came from copying *jumeau,* antique French and European dolls.

Although this Japanese look is now known as Goth-Loli, that term did not become popular until around the end of 1999 or 2000. It's not clear who came up with this moniker. Perhaps it began in a small Western-style clothes shop in Osaka and was taken up by other clothiers to describe this new look as "Gothic and Lolita-like." In Tokyo, the Goth-Loli trend first appeared in Harajuku, popularized by the many young girls who gathered next to Harajuku station on Jingu-bashi each Sunday for Hokoten, a weekly event where "visual-style" bands performed.

These Goth-Loli girls were photographed in the fashion magazine *KERA,* at which I worked as editor-in-chief. *KERA* started out in 1998 as a publication that aimed to introduce the richly individualistic fashions seen in Harajuku. Each month we spent ten days gathering images and information on the latest fashion trends. We noticed this movement growing bigger, so in December 2000 we published the "Gothic & Lolita Bible" as a *KERA* special issue. It became a huge hit, beyond our expectations, and sold out in three days. Eventually the trend made its way overseas, where it gained a following, and the expression "Gothic & Lolita" (or Goth-Loli for short) went on to become a byword not only domestically but internationally, particularly with the *anime* crowds and the *cosplay* (costume-play) set.

Around this same time, designers in Tokyo began to produce Goth-Loli clothes. Mana started his own brand, Moi-même-Moitié, in 1999, and in 2000 the brand h.NAOTO launched. h.NAOTO was the first Gothic brand able to expand nationwide. It started out as part of the company S-inc., which already had success with another brand and had outlets established across the country. The designer, Naoto Hirooka, was from Kansai and studied Western clothing design in Tokyo before he joined S-inc. Having worked his way up in the company, learning everything from the basics of making clothes to sales, he was noticed by the president. It was the president's support that gave Hirooka his start. Hirooka, like many other designers, admired and took inspiration from the powerful statements of Comme des Garçons. He was very talented, and produced designs in, but also beyond, the Goth-Loli style. Soon his clothes became internationally famous.

KERA was the first magazine to introduce this label and was inundated with phone calls asking where these clothes could be sourced. Because there were shops all over Japan where one could buy h.NAOTO clothing, and because the flamboyant band members inspired so many followers, Gothic clothes began to fly off the shelves all over the country. (There are currently five h.NAOTO stores in Harajuku alone and fourteen nationwide.) Not only were top Japanese musicians like Gackt and Hyde wearing h.NAOTO clothes, its reputation had even spread overseas, where famous musicians like Marilyn Manson were fans. Whenever Manson came to Japan he always stopped by the store. Amy Lee of the band Evanescence wore h.NAOTO clothing at a party after she won a Grammy, photographs of which were seen worldwide.

H.NAOTO was not the only important Goth-Loli label. Around 2000, in Harajuku, the SEX POT ReVeNGe brand started. Then, Hide and Taka, a designer duo, launched a popular line of T-shirts that had been spotted with dye and bleach and featured rebellious messages in Japanese. This heralded the arrival of Gothic & Punk, a sort of dirty and foul-mouthed addition to Gothic style. This punkish fad was fostered and spread by street kids who soon began setting up small shops in the backstreets of Harajuku.

Established Tokyo-based clothing companies jumped on the bandwagon and began to launch their own Gothic brands, such as Black Peace Now and Algonquins, to sell nationwide. With their experienced staff and larger factories, they made solid clothes of good quality, and with stores throughout Japan, it was easy for them to market their clothes. Although not strictly a Goth-Loli brand, Baby, The Stars Shine Bright, which started in 1989, was definitely Lolita: its fairytale-like clothes were a riot of pinks, light blues, whites, and other pastels rather than Gothic black. In the 2004 movie *Kamikaze Girls,* actress Kyoko Fukada wore the brand's clothes in every scene, raising awareness of the brand and the Lolita style and increasing its fan base.

Today, for the magazine *KERA Maniax,* I travel throughout the West, to America, the U.K., France, Germany, and Amsterdam, shooting pictures of people who embody the Gothic style. These fashion movements—Gothic, Goth-Lolita, and Lolita—are no longer just a Kansai or Harajuku phenomenon. So, the gothic movement that began in Japan in 1997 and spread with the publication of the *Gothic & Lolita Bible* has influenced style all over the world. I am often told by women who copy the Goth-Loli style, "Although we are imitating Japanese style we aren't as stylish as Japanese girls," even though originally the whole fashion trend was based on a Japanese longing for a European style. For us Japanese, while we might be happy to hear this, it's also slightly embarrassing.

Gothic and Lolita fashion, inspired by a yearning for something romantic overseas, was born in western Japan, Kansai, then moved up to Tokyo where it came of age, and after taking on the name "Harajuku Fashion," ended up travelling overseas, while, one must admit, remaining a slightly strange fashion indigenous to Japan.

KERA, KERA MANIAX, GOTHIC & LOLITA BIBLE
ケラ, ケラ マニアックス, ゴシックアンド ロリータバイブル

Started as a street-snap magazine, *KERA*'s original title was "KEROUAC"—a tangential reference to the author's *On the Road*. This magazine was launched in 1998, the year after another prominent street-snap magazine, *FRUiTS*. Shortened to *KERA* in 2000, the magazine's focus on music-related fashion combined documentary-style photographs of the burgeoning, flamboyant independent designer culture in Harajuku, which included fantasy and cyber brands like Fötus, W<, and Cyberdog, with the more girlish, punk-inspired brands also seen in *CUTiE*. Established brands such as Milk and Ba-tsu gained new currency in the way that the magazine presented their clothes mixed in with newer brands, and worn in different ways.

As the popularity of visual-kei bands gained momentum—producing a new crop of influential stars—so did the need for a magazine that reflected the culture and fashion that was a world apart from the commercial market prevalent at the time. *Gothic & Lolita Bible* was launched in 2000 initially as a special issue of *KERA,* and it was the first magazine dedicated to this intermingling of Gothic and Lolita

クスMOOK
ERA
マニアックス
コラボ通販
BABY, THE STARS SHINE BRIGHTが
作る「マリー・アントワネット」服ほか
マニアックス
MANIAX
マニアックス7.8スペシャル
SPECIAL
ロイヤル×パンク
ONDON
ンドン塔物語
ハリーポッター」の
ンドン
ド・ヴィシャスの
UNKロンドン完全ガイド
ンドンでお買い物&観光♥
くっても★
くっても
プレゼント
003-2006
WORLD
NAP
520
★LONDON
★PARIS
★NY★東京
★GERMANY
ロココなカバーガール
土屋アンナ
映画
「NANA 2」
ファッション解剖
ナナ服PRESENT!
旅する
深田恭子ちゃん
海賊★CAスタイル
宝野アリカ
「パリ旅行物語」
Mana interview
ロリータちゃんの
ぬりえ
三原ミツカズ
はやかわともこ
ゴシック×ロリータ
PARIS
★マリー・アントワネット
★「ダ・ヴィンチ・コード」の
★ロココな貴族の館めぐり
★パリ観光ガイド
+モンサンミシェル
東京+大阪
ショップガイド
ロリータちゃんなら絶対行きたい!
★ロリータカフェ★執事喫茶
★ゴシックカフェ…
★★★おしゃれカフェガイド★★★
★ディズニーランド+ディズニーシーガイド

styles, as well as Lolita fashion itself. Its regular features included photographs of Mana (the performer/musician credited with first combining the Goth and Lolita styles), articles on Goth style history and Goth-Loli hair and makeup tips, and clothes from brands such as Metamorphose temps de fille, Victorian maiden, and Black Peace Now.

KERA Maniax was launched in 2003 with a focus on even darker clothing and international style points and references, such as features on the life and art of Lewis Carroll, Japanese ball-joint dolls, or interviews with icons like Courtney Love (a *KERA Maniax* reader and fan). But somehow, *KERA Maniax*'s covers still manage to make dark and Gothic look cute.

Pages 138–139: 2007 issues of *KERA*, *KERA Maniax*, and *Gothic & Lolita Bible*. *Opposite:* "Flower Fairies" make the Goth Loli scene (*top*); More *KERA*, including covers playing on Vivienne Westwood's penchant for pirate gear; and the October, 2003 issue of featuring Amy Lee from Evanescence on the cover (*bottom right*). *This page: KERA Maniax* cover models Anna Tsuchiya (*top left*) and Kyoko Fukuda (*bottom right*) from the film *Kamikaze Girls*; *Gothic & Lolita Bible* covers featuring illustrations from popular manga (*top right*); and the 1998 debut issue of *Kerouac*, featuring the sell-copy "For Excentric Boys and Girls" (*bottom left*).

BABY, THE STARS SHINE BRIGHT

ベイビー、ザスターズシャインブライト

Akinori Isobe started Baby, The Stars Shine Bright (commonly referred to as simply "Baby") in 1988 after working at Atsuki Onishi's design office. Onishi, Baby, and the Lolita movement were influenced by designer Isao Kaneko (see *An An*) and his romantic Victorian-meets-*Little-House-on-the-Prairie*-style outfits that were lovely, pink, and ruffled. In the early days, Isobe explains, they struggled to find a brand identity that stood out on the racks. A quick fix was discovered in the addition of lace and ribbons. Lots of them. The clothes became so decorative that the Baby team themselves were unsure who might buy such over-the-top confections. But, Baby had found a silhouette that was a playful and abundant contrast to the form-fitted, sleek body-con aesthetic that was popular internationally. Just as Baby had found their aesthetic voice, the visual-kei band boom came to life in Osaka in 1997. With the bands' female fans eager to dress as decoratively as their idols, Baby's bloomers and aprons with heart-shaped pockets were the rage. Lolita fashion also gained traction as a subculture with the increasing popularity of the Internet, with girls interested in *cosplay* and *manga* starting in 1996. Featuring a character dressed in Lolita fashion, the 2004 film *Shimotsuma Monogatari* (released with the English title *Kamikaze Girls*) helped push the style still further into the mainstream. In early 2007, Baby opened a boutique in Paris's Bastille district and counts Courtney Love as one of its international fans.

Baby, The Stars Shine Bright is one of the most influential Lolita brands. The brand name was plucked from the lyrics of the group Everything But the Girl. Pictured here are images from Baby's A/W 2007 catalogue. ***Opposite, below:*** A still from the film *Kamikaze Girls* (2004) with actress Kyoko Fukada. The film fueled domestic interest in Lolita fashion—the wardrobe was by Baby, and a character was named after Baby owner Akinori Isobe.

BRI
BABY

しもつま
下妻
SHIMOTSUMA
だいほう
そうどう
学生割引・パック料金制度有り
公認
県西自動車学校
関城町船玉286
☎0296−37−6012代
大型・大特
普通
けん引
大型二輪
普通二輪
boutique

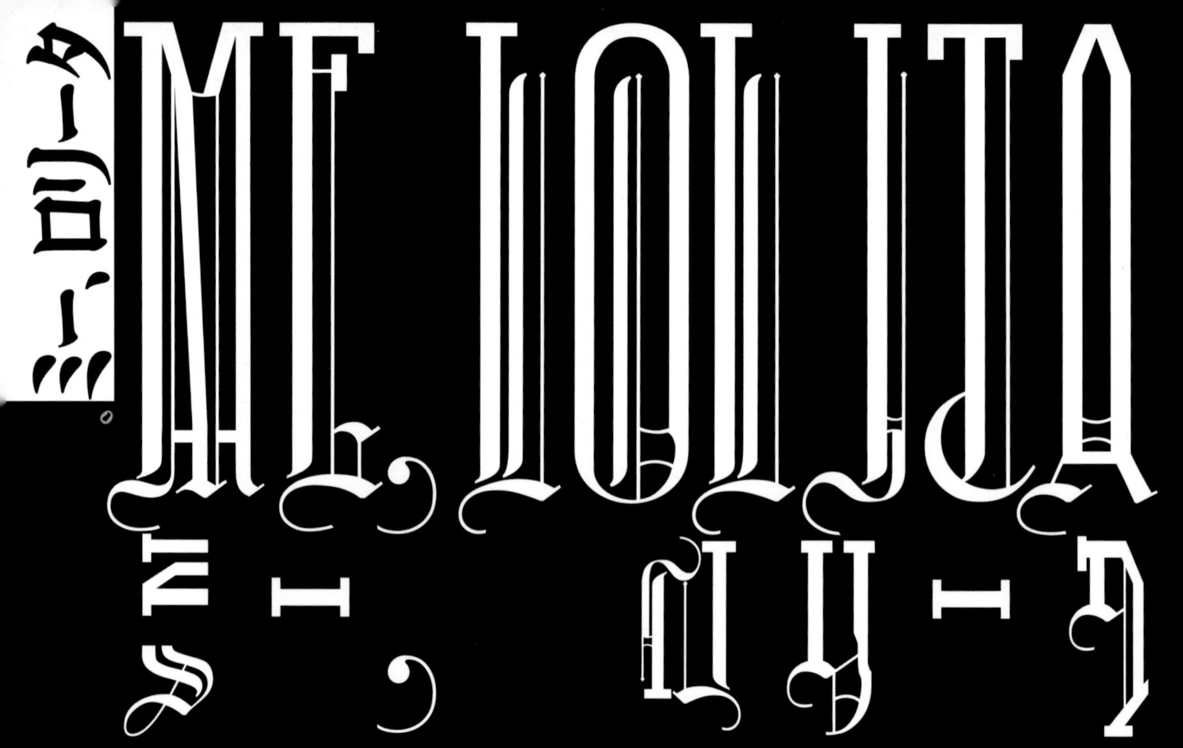

Dressing in frills and lace can look like or feel like a costume, but for Raine, Lolita-style clothing is her regular, daily wear, and even lifestyle. Twenty-two years old, she is an employee at the shop Baby, The Stars Shine Bright.

You don't have a typical name.

Raine is the name I use at work. It's a leftover from my visual-kei days.

When did you start wearing this style?

I started in junior high school, 1996–97. I was into visual-kei bands at the time, but they are all so minor you wouldn't know them. I wanted to find really cute clothing. And then *wow!* I found this cute Lolita style. I love the frills, the lace, the ribbons. They look like doll clothes. From the first glance [*placing both hands over her chest and gasping slightly*] it's so cute. Some of us like strawberry prints and ribbons more than others. It's about being completely absorbed in your own world. Even down to the shoes.

Do the stares and teasing bother you?

People are mean to me sometimes and they take pictures of me as if I am Minnie Mouse or some tourist attraction. It's annoying that normal people say things to me. Why do you have a right to say things to me when you look like *that?* If this were the eighteenth century, this dress would be totally normal. Some girls are into early American looks, like pilgrims. Bonnets and everything. Do you get it? That's what we like. It's simple.

How would you describe the type of girl who becomes a Lolita?

She is very independent. She is not going to get a boyfriend wearing these clothes. For Lolitas, fantasy is better than reality. Seeing someone in concert, for example, is an image of perfection. All made up and dressed to the nines, a living doll—Lolitas find that much more appealing than putting up with some guy who complains. The guys in bands are beautiful. *Akogareru wo yuruseru.* [Roughly meaning, "It's OK to pursue your dreams."] But in real life and with real guys, there are too many things to deal with. This generation—girls in their mid-twenties now—is no longer pressured to get married and have children. Lolitas enjoy living alone, enjoy being surrounded by cute things, creating their own worlds.

Tell me about Lolita interests and hobbies.

We are interested in getting away from reality and living in our own world. We like reading Goth-Lolita-themed *manga*. I don't think this could happen in America. The way people think in America is free. You can lead life the way you want and have the hobbies you want. But that's not the case in Japan. On my day off I like to go shopping around Harajuku, to visit my friends that work in stores. Or else I stay home and drink my favorite tea. We will get together with friends and have tea and sandwiches. I love cake because it goes well with tea. I like ballet and opera. My home is not a castle, but I try to decorate it and create my own atmosphere. I have a lot of white furniture. Antique-looking furniture. Lots of ribbons around the room. I read about Lolita and listen to Lolita-type music. I like reading *KERA* and *Gothic & Lolita Bible*. I would love to go to Germany to see an actual castle. I've never been abroad.

What would you pack?

What I would normally wear. A lot of people look at me but this is how I am.

Who's your favorite musician now?

Kanoma-san (Kanoma). The is the vocalist of the visual-kei band Fatima.

What do you want out of life?

I am happy as I am. There are older people that come into the store. Even when I get older I'll continue living this life.

Raine is a typical "living doll." She is photographed here across the street from her favorite shop, Daikanyama's Baby, The Stars Shine Bright, where she is also part of the shop staff. The look that she models here, including all its layers and accessories, cost her about 90,000 yen (around US$900).

エイチナオト

H.NAOTO
エイチナオト

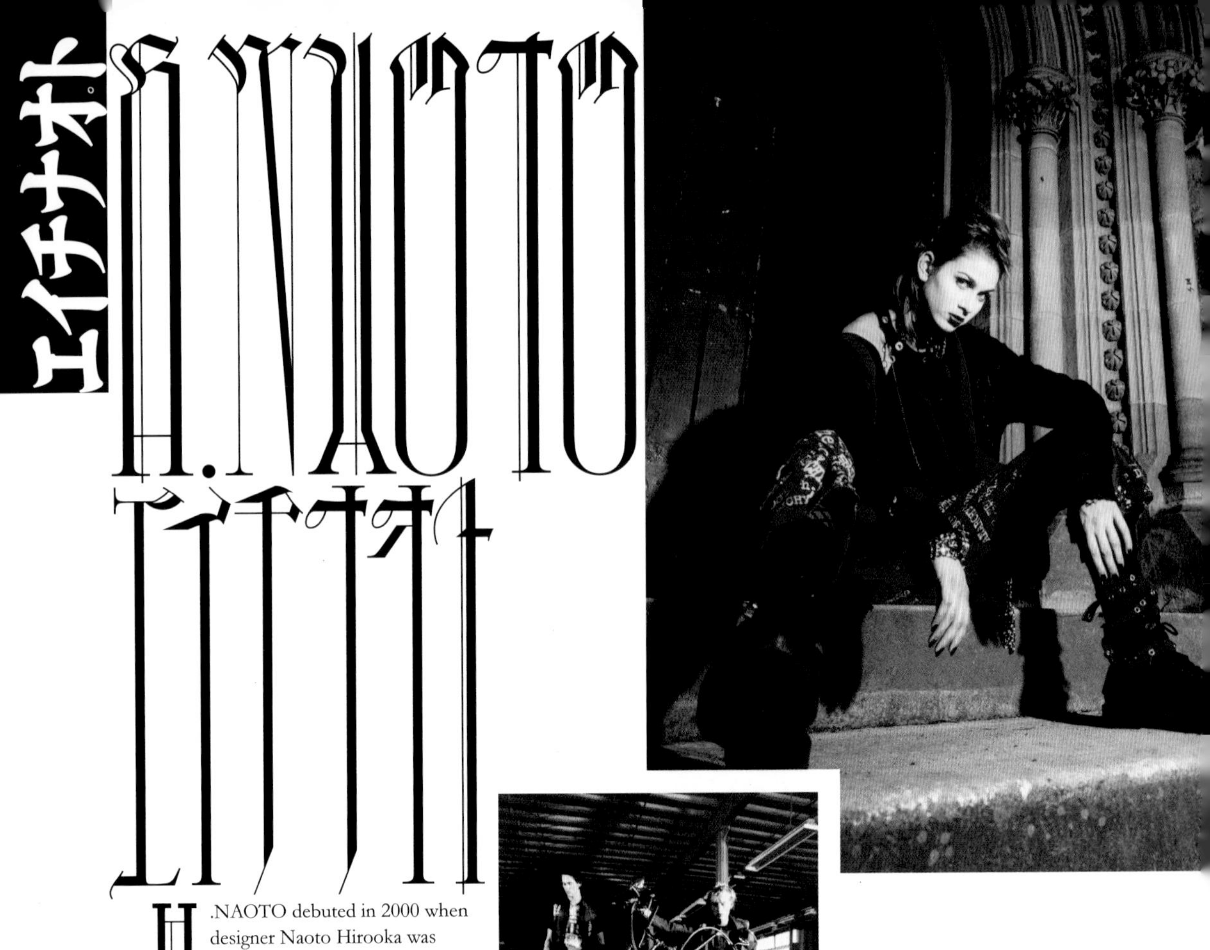

H.NAOTO debuted in 2000 when designer Naoto Hirooka was only twenty-two—backed by S-inc., which had also enjoyed success with the vintage remake brand T. Kunitomo. Bunka Fashion College graduate Hirooka is one of the most successful designers to surface from the Gothic or Lolita movements. His dramatic punk- and rock-influenced clothes are favored by Japanese and foreign musicians alike. (Evanescence vocalist Amy Lee wore one of his dresses at the 49th Annual Grammy Awards, and Marilyn Manson bought out the entire store on a trip to Tokyo.)

Totally tapped into the hearts of punk fashion–loving Lolitas, Hirooka has expanded his collection with several new lines and concept store offshoots. CHANNEL H draws on *cosplay* and *anime* influences. Hanging from the ceiling of the gallery-like shop hEAVEN is clothing that makes references to Comme des Garçons, while still being punkish and Lolita. Also on display are Hangry and Angry, two cute but bloodied stuffed toy characters Hirooka created. The 8 Club concept shop is girly and sexy, while h. is a men's store with military- and street- and hip-hop-inspired brands all designed by Hirooka. h.NAOTO Rooms is an interior design shop. (Imagine Versace's Home collection mixed with death metal flare.)

Opposite top and middle, this page bottom right and left: The industrial settings of h.NAOTO's 2004 advertising images, shot on location in Australia, accentuate the rock and rough side of the brand. *Opposite left and top: Edward Scissorhands*, visual-kei, and sci-fi inspired images from the 2006 campaign.

セックスポットリベンジ

SEX POT REVENGE

Trashlight Vision

The defining element for visual-kei bands is the use of presentation as much as music to express themselves. Garish makeup and freakish costumes are the norm for these bands, while the music is dark and creepy. SEX POT ReVeNGe is a favorite of such bands, including Antique Café and 12012 as well as Philadelphia's punk band Trashlight Vision. The brand's clothing is part of the stage performance. This is a ready-to-wear line for the stage. Such an overt link between music and fashion was also employed by Vivienne Westwood and Malcolm McLaren and their line Seditionaries of the '70s, which the Sex Pistols wore on stage. In Japan, *cosplay* (short for "costume play," meaning dressing up like one's favored musician or icon) is a widely practiced recreation. This makes brands like SEX POT ReVeNGe, which have strong connections with music scenes, a fascinating mixture of fashion and culture. Instead of fans sewing their own versions of stagewear, the clothing is available for purchase.

Visual-kei now encompasses a broad range of sub-styles that are less sinister—punkish or pop and cute. There are androgynous boy bands or modish punks that look like cocktails of the Sex Pistols, Cream Soda, and a splash of Boy George. If you are a musician or just want to look like one, SEX POT ReVeNGe is your brand.

SEX POT ReVeNGe's free quarterly music magazine, *Vinyl Syndicate*, features portraits of bands in the brand's clothes, including New York punk band Trashlight Vision (***opposite, top***), and the visual-kei band 12012 (***opposite, bottom***) and Antique Café (***above***). ***This page, left:*** Harajuku shop staffer Megu models a look put together from elements of the Summer 2007 collection.

LINDA BRIDGE

PHOTOGRAPHY BY KAI REGAN

Mana, here dressed in his trademark look for his band Malice Mizer, which was the start of Gothic Lolita fashion.

There's nothing peculiar about idolizing one's heroes, such as fans idolizing music stars. In Harajuku, this idolatry isn't limited to musicians. Designers, stylists, hairdressers, and photographers also enjoy the limelight. It's a Cult of Image. For example, to an entire generation of youth, tastemaker extraordinaire Hiroshi Fujiwara represents the connection between *otaku** sensibilities and hip-hop and numerous other fields of pop culture, and in this regard he has something like rock-star status. All segments of Harajuku have their celebrities who set trends or, more generally, function as influencers. In Japan, such influencers have a palpable effect on public opinion and directly impact the market.

One of the prime celebrities and influencers of the Goth-Loli world, Mana, is a hybrid between music celebrity and fashion designer. Currently the lead guitarist and songwriter for the band Moi dix Mois (after the breakup of Malice Mizer in 2001), he is also the band's artistic director, choreographing their on-stage performance interludes (usually without musical accompaniment) and, more important, their wardrobe. Moi dix Mois is one of the key visual-kei bands, part of a larger genre of musical acts that have a very stylized look. The closest Western example (but still falling short) is the band Kiss. Big hair. Layers of makeup. Signature costumes. But while Kiss is a heavy metal band, visual-kei bands like X JAPAN, Color, Dead End, and L'Erlanger are by and large a cross between metal, punk, goth, cyber, and rock. The sounds are hard, and the looks are dark and severe. While some Kiss fans may paint their faces like the band when attending concerts, in Harajuku fans have an entire wardrobe, based on their favorite visual-kei bands, that they wear every day. One of the major labels of this genre is Mana's own brand, Moi-même-Moitié (MmM).

Of these visual-kei bands, there are a number of superstars, like Gackt (now a solo artist after a stint in Malice Mizer, another band for which Mana was the main artistic director and songwriter). Mana launched MmM after Malice Mizer disbanded, and his new band's music, by Mana's own description, comes from the image that he is projecting. The closest articulations of this image are represented in the spirit of two avatars Mana has created, Elegant Gothic Aristocrat (E.G.A.) and Elegant Gothic Lolita (E.G.L.), which represent his ideals. Mana's description of E.G.A. is confounding: "It is either male or female but it is also neither male nor female. It is both devil and angel. The pursuit of a middle ground." While E.G.L. is modeled on a young girl, she is not much closer to reality. Embellished with ribbons and bows, E.G.L. is meant to be "like an antique doll with a dark spirit."

Mana's involvement with designing outfits came from his live performances, and the clothing began as costumes that made their way into the audience and everyday life. Mana's image is a combination of Gothic and Lolita styles; that he brought together the styles in a music context dramatically increased its appeal.

In the Goth-Loli style, we see the flourishing of the female *otaku,* who prefer their own obsessive world of interests to reality at large. The vast majority of Mana's fans are young women, just as one would expect the majority of Goth-Loli dressers to be female. While, in the West, lace and stockings and maid's uniforms are highly sexualized, in Japan the Goth-Loli style is worn without any erotic charge. While it may be natural to associate "Lolita" with Nabokov's novel and title character, there is no connection intended here. The term is a signifier displaced. Lolita style in Japan is demure, not one of the child-vamp, and embodies a hyperstylized, lacy vision of femininity. Similarly, in the visual-kei context, men dressing as women is less a form of gender bending or cross-dressing than it is a form of costuming and roleplay.

The Goth-Loli image is an amalgam of *Phantom of the Opera, Alice in Wonderland,* and Edgar Allan Poe, with Alice Cooper on vocals and Beethoven on keyboards. It appropriates culture and periods in a mismatched way akin to the surreal logic of a dream, at a remove from the mundane. As Mana offers, "The performance is up to you."

**Otaku,* or, *o-taku,* means "home" and was originally used as slang to describe a generation of young people in Japan who were basically shut-ins. Their preoccupation with *manga, anime,* and other fantasy worlds to the exclusion of interacting with people was frowned upon, and incidents of homicide that involved teenage *otaku* cast the issue as a social problem in the early 1990s. Since then, the term has come to mean almost anyone who has a great degree of knowledge about any one particular field. It still carries the nuance of social ineptitude.

This page: Mana dressed in two personas, E.G.L. (left) and E.G.A. (right). *Opposite:* True to visual-kei style, Malice Mizer and Mana's current band Moi dix Mois incorporates theatrical performances into their live shows.

GODisDEAD

URA-HARA HARAJUKU

裏原

URA-HARA

In 1982, before product design was on my plate, I came to Japan to hand-shape surfboards in the country, far away from Tokyo. On the way out of Japan I would float around Harajuku, shopping and absorbing the bubbling vibe of street culture. As a guy exposed to the gluttony of the U.S., I loved all the old ways of Japanese culture. While exploring Tokyo I stumbled onto early Comme des Garçons and Yohji Yamamoto, and I also enjoyed the Japanese take on our classic American feeling. I was intrigued by what I saw. The opportunity to do something new, or at least combine stuff with a fresh viewpoint, was sparked in me then and there. I will always have a special place in my heart for Harajuku.

—Shawn Stussy

HARAJUKU®

URA-HARA, HIP HOP, PUNK, D.I.Y.

UNDERGROUND TAKES OVERGROUND

by Tetsuya Suzuki

Though Harajuku is a small district within Tokyo, it contains numerous sub-sections that have grown up around a handful of shops or designers. One such sub-section is Ura-Hara. A contraction of Ura-Harajuku (*ura* means "behind" or "under"), the term both refers to the backstreets of Harajuku and is used to contrast Ura-Hara with Omotesando (*omote* means "top" or "above"). So, Ura-Hara is the alter-ego of Harajuku's glitzy side. Where Harajuku is frenetic and gaudy and exhibitionist, Ura-Hara is reserved, almost monochromatic in palette, and hidden. There is also a clear gender split between the two. Ura-Hara's domain is that of male designers and their exclusively male market, guys of a generation that rejected the empty commercialization of 1980s fashion subcultures and DC-brand, mass-produced imitations of Western styles. It emerged around the efforts of Hiroshi Fujiwara (who designs for numerous labels), BAPE (A Bathing Ape), and UNDER COVER, which cater to a certain type of masculine

Ura-Hara's domain is that of male designers and their exclusively male market, guys of a generation that rejected the empty commercialization of 1980s fashion subcultures and DC-brand, mass-produced imitations of Western styles.

**アンチテーゼとしては80年代的なサブカルチャー、
ニューウェーブが商業化していった部分、
とくにファッションにおける「DCブランド」と呼ばれた
欧米のコピースタイルをブランド化し、
国内向けに拡大生産するという
ビジネスモデルの否定である。**

Hiroshi Fujiwara parlayed this network of contacts into a considerable sphere of influence over Tokyo's street culture in the late 1980s. With his attenuated radar picking up the latest trends and information, Fujiwara became Tokyo's go-to authority on youth culture, garnering the attention of all media watchers.

interest in fashion, music (mostly hip-hop), graffiti, and skater culture. The Ura-Hara movement is an amalgam of all these subcultures.

Hiroshi Fujiwara is recognized by everyone involved in Harajuku as the progenitor of Ura-Hara. Fujiwara has seemingly always been someone in-the-know. When he was a teenager in the 1980s, he started his career as a DJ in the Tokyo club scene—hanging out with the Plastics and others connected with the band. He parlayed this network of contacts into a considerable sphere of influence over Tokyo's street culture in the late 1980s. With his attenuated radar picking up the latest trends and information, Fujiwara became Tokyo's go-to authority on youth culture, garnering the attention of all media watchers. For street kids who were seeking edgy culture, he was someone they could look up to, who was exposed to numerous subcultures abroad, and, most important, someone who was an entrepreneur living "the life." Because of his position at the center of things, Fujiwara set the stage for a number of other designers to follow, thus setting into motion what would become the Ura-Hara movement. These included creators like A Bathing Ape's Nigo, UNDER COVER's Jun Takahashi, and Neighborhood's Nobusuke Takizawa, all of whom were part of this crowd of young Fujiwara followers.

The Ura-Hara movement effectively became recognizable with Nigo and Jonio's opening of the Nowhere shop in 1993, along the backstreets of Harajuku.

Ura-Hara as a movement effectively became recognized with Nigo and Jonio's opening of the Nowhere shop in 1993, along the backstreets of Harajuku. Typical of Tokyo, most of the streets in the area are narrow, unnamed, curving, winding, end abruptly, or cross each other in oddly formed intersections, giving shops and buildings a feeling of being tucked away and below the radar. This physical reality helped reinforce the idea that the store was doing something in a new and different way. The fact that the Ura-Hara designers at first couldn't afford to advertise like established brands was used to their advantage, with A Bathing Ape and UNDER COVER "leaking" information to the media, often to the same magazines in which these designers had regular columns. The clothes were made in limited editions, which further added to their allure. It's not clear whether the designers limited availability in order to create a frenzy or not, but the fact is, their guerrilla-marketing tactics led to commercial success. They were seen as mysterious, and their clothes were seen as an entrée into a highly sophisticated lifestyle that emerged from a fusion of punk, skater, and biker street cultures. This street-based lifestyle was authentic Tokyo style, which these kids developed by taking elements of culture from overseas and mixing and combining them with their own original ideas. To be a part of it and own one of these limited articles of clothing, kids had to have their ear to the ground to learn about new items in time. Then they would wait in line before the shops opened to get their hands on a new design.

80年代後半に入り、
藤原ヒロシはますますフットワークを早め、
影響力の範囲を広げる。
具体的には、ストリートカルチャーにとどまらない
ワールドワイドな人脈と誰よりも感度の高いアンテナで、
国内外の情報をほぼリアルタイムで
雑誌メディアなどに紹介するという「役目」を
引き受けることになる。

Since 2000, each of the original Ura-Hara creators has been developing and expanding these brands. UNDER COVER recently moved into women's runway fashion, showing in Paris. A Bathing Ape has been growing in tandem with hip-hop culture and is enjoying international recognition in that scene, especially in the U.S. And Neighborhood has developed a uniquely sophisticated urban casual style with street elements that has garnered industry attention and many overseas fans. Each label has moved away from being summed up by the term "Ura-Hara," and has begun to take on its own identity even outside of Japan. As they establish independence, it is likely they will follow in the footsteps of Comme des Garçons, the predecessor to the new generation of Japanese fashion.

自己表現の方法を
「ファッション」に定めた
彼らの新しい
「やり方」が始まる。
その象徴が
NOWHEREの
オープンである。

Each label has
moved away from being
summed up
by the term "Ura-Hara,"
and has begun to take
on its own identity
even outside of Japan.

Hiroshi Fujiwara on the February 2004 cover of *HUGE* magazine.

HIROSHI FUJIWARA

ヒロシ フジワラ

Hiroshi Fujiwara's range of activity spans from DJing in new wave clubs in Tokyo in the 1980s, writing a column about trends in the United States and Europe for cutting-edge lifestyle magazines, designing both clothes and shops, working as a stylist for photo shoots, and recording music. He has designed or art directed for numerous high-profile clients, including designing sneakers for Nike and denim clothing for Levis. He has also collaborated with Eric Clapton and art directed a DVD release. But perhaps, Fujiwara can best be appreciated for his role in connecting people, starting trends, and helping a whole generation of young Japanese men to discover (for example) hip-hop.

Fujiwara has been recognized for his talent as a tastemaker since the early 1980s. Clocking serious amounts of time in the West (he would occasionally return to Tokyo for moneymaking stints, such as DJing at fashion shows), he gathered firsthand information on a range of cultural movements and trends and brought early word back to Tokyo on everything from punk to hip-hop to graffiti art to sneaker culture. His magazine columns tracking the hottest trends in the West helped make him a media icon, and through his connections with retailers, designers, and other media producers, he was able to introduce foreign cultural trends directly into Japan. He was the international filter for anything that was cool or new. And although it wasn't always the case that everyone heeded his enthusiasms (some fashionistas found it hard to take streetwear seriously), his influence continued to grow to the point that today just the hint of acknowledgment from him of a certain sound, style, or trend can launch a boom. Certainly it is this cachet that makes large companies want to use him as a designer or consultant.

His first expedition abroad was in 1982, when at eighteen he went to London to explore the music and culture scene. He wound up working briefly at World's End, the shop that Vivienne Westwood and Malcolm McLaren created to sell a range of ready-to-wear items, which all tended to be fantastical in design. At McLaren's prompting, Fujiwara went to New York. In the early 1990s he became excited by Los Angeles' skate culture, particularly by the work of Stüssy. Like Stüssy, Fujiwara's streetwear designs and promotions mixed punk style with skate culture with hip-hop. His kinship and later association with Shawn Stussy and also with designer Michael Koppleman from Gimme Five in London were pivotal as these designers helped bring Japanese street fashion to the rest of the world by promoting and selling Japanese brands.

In 2000, Fujiwara closed a shop called Ready Made, where he sold his own designs (which he also distributed through his friends' shops). Unusual for the fashion industry, he would also make and release T-shirts without taking credit for them. He wanted people to appreciate them for their design, not for his name. That said, it became the ultimate in-the-know test to be able to identify and buy an "unsigned" Fujiwara before they were all snapped up. His preference for short-term projects and the freedom they give him to move on to the next thing—the reason he never started his own brand—coupled with an air of mystery about his activities, adds to his allure and the hype surrounding him. He wants to stay underground, but is at the same time the most *over*ground, visible person on the

Japanese street fashion scene. This is part of the mystery. Other designers, like Nigo and Jonio, are known for their labels—BAPE and UNDER COVER, respectively—whereas Fujiwara is known simply for being Fujiwara.

In 2002, Fujiwara started a project with Nike, launching HTM, a limited-edition line of sneakers. It was to be the first of many projects together, iconic in that it was one of the first instances of Harajuku limited-edition culture being incorporated into a big-business paradigm. As Fujiwara explains, "The whole idea of limited edition is about image, and no one makes money off it. The people that make money are the people who resell it." The real money in limited editions comes in the resale market, but the cool factor it contributes to a brand is incalculable. The limited edition is now a frequently used marketing strategy.

Below, left: Silk-screen portrait of Marx, circa 1990, printed by Jun Takahashi and Hiroshi Fujiwara for their collaboration brand AFFA. **Below:** Military jacket AFFA MA-1 CUSTOM.

Clockwise from top: 2002 NIKE AIR FORCE 1 LOW W+K TOKYO EDT; HTM AIR MOC MID; 2002 AIR WOVEN BOOT prototype.

Top, middle left, bottom right: Martin Acoustic Guitar #839775 EC+HF Custom-Made, 2002, manufactured by Martin & Co., Customized by Eric Clapton and Hiroshi Fujiwara. *Middle right:* Eric Clapton USA Tour jacket by GOODENOUGH. *Bottom left:* HEAD PORTER+PLUS parka designed by Eric Clapton and Hiroshi Fujiwara. *Opposite:* Burton Snowboard Decks "Nu Project," 2001, manufactured by Burton Snowboards, graphic design by Hiroshi Fujiwara.

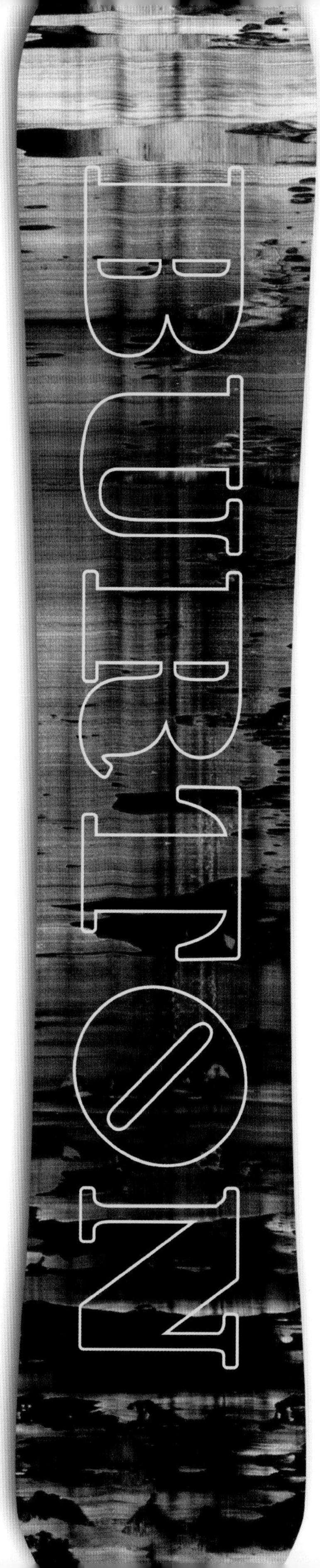

There is a strong and influential link between Harajuku and Asia, and now the world and Harajuku. It is something that we can call our own when you talk about Asia. For the Asian kids, the people that design fashion in Harajuku represent our whole feeling. The quality is high. I think especially in Hong Kong, there is this Japanese craze with fashion. It is more about this exclusivity. This way you don't have to join a club, don't need anyone's approval, you just need to get that shirt! A lot of young Asians see this type of clothing as status. In the States, somebody will buy a T-shirt from Abercrombie and be happy with it. I don't see that happening in Asia. Harajuku is a culture. It is so many things. The people that come from Harajuku don't only do fashion: some make music, they DJ, some are fighters in the circuit now, but they also influence music, and electronics. What's cool in Tokyo and Japan, and then Asia, is based on these people. When Hiroshi uses a phone, he doesn't have to say it's good, he just takes a picture of it for his column and it ends up in a magazine and that is the next hot phone. Does that have anything to do with fashion? Kind of, but it goes into a different realm. I think that there is definitely a whole culture that follows this, the way you walk, the way you talk, your taste. It is kind of like hip-hop, you can't just say it is music, 'cause it has so many other different things to it. Harajuku culture is the same.

—Edison Chen

Above: Porter Record Bag in collaboration with GOODENOUGH, mid-1990s, manufactured by Yoshida Co., Ltd. *Bottom left:* GOODENOUGH "Big Eighth Note" T-shirt, early 1990s. *Right:* GOODENOUGH Gretsch G-brand Guitar Motif T-shirt, early 1990s. *Opposite, top:* GOODENOUGH "End Racism" T-shirt, 1991. *Below:* A design collaboration between Supreme and GOODENOUGH, late 1990s.

SUPRODENOUGH

SUPRODENOUGH

SUPRODENOUGH

NYLON
guys
Bape's
Nigo:
The Man
Behind
The Bling
The Evolution
of Queens of
the Stone Age
PLUS
Mark Ronson
Cisco Adler
Shia LaBeouf
+ so long,
Sopranos
Sophia
Bush
gets our
vote!
WWW.GUYS.NYLONMAG.COM
$3.99US $4.99CAN
0 74470 02031 8
NERD

A BATHING APE

ア ベイシング エイプ

BAPE is on a steady course to becoming an empire. Of all the Ura-Hara brands, BAPE (an abbreviation of A Bathing Ape) has enjoyed the greatest notoriety and crossover into the American, U.K. and Asian markets. Its numerous sub-brands and businesses cover everything from women's and children's wear to sneakers, a record studio, a record label, hair salons, and an art gallery. Behind it all is BAPE's art director and sole proprietor, Nigo.

While he was working as an editor and stylist in the early 1990s for the magazine *Popeye,* Nigo opened a shop, Nowhere, with Jonio, who would later become the designer of UNDER COVER, another brand to rise out of Ura-Hara. Their shop's name underscored many aspects of the Ura-Hara style, which, in contrast to Harajuku, avoided attention-grabbing storefronts and flashy advertising. The selection of merchandise at the shop was also low-key, carrying Jonio's original T-shirts and a sampling of Nigo's American paraphernalia (sneakers, figures, used clothing), which they were more interested in displaying than selling. Essentially, Nigo is a collector, and his activities with BAPE have grown out of this. His Tokyo penthouse, for instance, used to house his collections of sneakers and *Star Wars* memorabilia. Nigo describes himself as a "cool *otaku,*" by which he makes a distinction between being a fan and being consumed by your obsessions/fixations.

Both Nigo and Jonio had their own pages in the lifestyle magazine *Takarajima* (thanks to Hitomi Okawa's introduction of them to the magazine's editor-in-chief), which certainly helped attract people to the shop. Because of this, their stock would sell out quickly. Since Nigo was working during the day as an editor and also sidelining at night as a DJ, he didn't have time to travel to the States to shop for new merchandise to keep the place stocked. Thus the next step was for him to start making his own items to sell, so in 1993 he started BAPE.

Nigo's involvement with DJ culture, and the fact that he grew up with the idea of using samples and remixing to create new music, led to his bringing this approach to fashion as well. Appropriation was his way of showing his appreciation for things he liked, such as sneakers and American pop culture, which he transformed and incorporated into his brand.

He was also a great fan of Hiroshi Fujiwara, the man responsible for initiating the Ura-Hara scene and introducing hip-hop to Japan. Fujiwara was the coolest kid around, in the eyes of the young men involved with music at the time. Soon Nigo and Fujiwara became friends. It also happened that they look alike, a fact that led to Nigo's name (in Japanese, *nigo* means "number two"). Nigo was the second Hiroshi Fujiwara.

Like Fujiwara, Nigo tapped into the zeitgeist of a rising, young male consciousness in Japan at that time. He was a media star. At that time, Ura-Hara brands were essentially things made by a small group of guys who were all friends, who made clothes for themselves and their circle, and who wanted to stay underground—which of course made them even cooler to those outside the club. The young men who bought their brands were buying into this cool club. The Ura-Hara creators know how much Japanese people flip out over exclusive items and *gentei mono* (limited-edition products). But in the beginning there was also a practical reality in producing "limited editions": they might only be able to afford to print fifty shirts, thirty of which would go to friends. With the small profits, Nigo might finance a run of jeans, and with that some shoes, and so on. He still follows this model today, offering just a few hundred pieces of each design, but also offering more different designs at one time.

Since 1999, when Nigo decided to take things *over*ground and separate himself from the brands that had become known as Ura-Hara, he transcended the boom created by all the media hype. He moved his store to Aoyama—a more mainstream district. Soon after, he collaborated with Pepsi, using the BAPE camouflage on the bottles. He started a record label and started doing BAPE events for his label. By going mainstream, Nigo turned BAPE into a lifestyle brand rather than a street- and clubwear label. He has opened a hair salon and a café, the kidswear boutique, and he hopes to open a hotel. Together with Pharrell Williams of the band the Neptunes, he started the Billionaire Boys Club and Ice Cream labels. While Fujiwara has avoided becoming strongly associated with any one brand, Nigo has done the opposite, locking himself into his brand image and thus entrenching himself in pop culture. His influence has also penetrated America. Nigo's designs transformed hip-hop's style. Now bad boys like Jay-Z, Kanye West, and Pharrell are wearing pink sneakers and T-shirts imprinted with monkey graphics and ice cream cones—hip-hop as hip pop.

Page 178: The million dollar man and his famous Jacob the Jeweler bling on the cover of American magazine *Nylon guys* (Summer 2007). *Below:* Examples of his genius packaging design, each of these products contains a T-shirt. No wonder people wait in line outside the store to get this stuff. *Opposite:* An iteration of A Bathing Ape's logo.

A BATHING APE®
BAPEXCLUSIVE®

Opposite: Flagship store Bapexclusive in Aoyama. Nigo worked with interior designer Katayama Masamichi to create boutiques that were unlike any other streetwear brands in Harajuku or otherwise. The idea of putting valuable collectibles—a rare comic book or action figure—in protective plastic housings was employed as an aesthetic, expanded and refined to make entire stores feel like a display case. Glass, steel, and tile gave the shops a cool, clinical feel instead of the rough-and-tumble casualness one would expect. ***Below:*** BAPE STA!! Pro-Wrestling Champion belt. BAPE collaboration with Hello Kitty (2005). ***Right:*** the package from the Pepsi campaign that took BAPE mainstream (2001). ***Bottom left:*** The BAPE CUTS salon. ***Bottom right:*** Bapexlusive's second floor with glass encased rotating shoe display case.

PEEL SLOWLY AND SEE

Cherie

BEEF OR CHICKEN
4+1
TERIYAKI BOYZ

Nigo's numerous collaborations include projects with Futura, KAWS, James Lavelle, and seen here the Beastie Boys (***opposite, bottom left***), figures were created and even styled by Nigo for the release of their 1998 album *Hello Nasty*. ***Opposite, top:*** KAWS art work decorates the cover of the limited edition album from Ape Sounds artist Cherie (2002). ***Opposite, bottom right:*** Nigo's latest pet project, the hip-hop crew The Teriyaki Boys' *Beef or Chicken* (2005), co-released by Def Jam Recordings and Ape Sounds. ***This page:*** Ice Cream sneakers for the Billionaire Boys Club brand Nigo collaborates on with Pharrell Williams.

SK8 THING

GRAPHIC DESIGN BY SK8THING

Ura-Hara muse and graphic artist, Sk8thing, first visited Garage Paradise Harajuku in 1978. Cream Soda's leopard-print-painted building, Garage Paradise's in-store DJ booth, and the area's all-around rock 'n' roll vibe left a deep impression on the preteen. After becoming involved in the hardcore and skateboarding scenes in the early 1980s, he soon hooked up with the emerging street culture celebrity Hiroshi Fujiwara (who was just a few years older than Sk8thing, but already had established himself on the scene) and they began to skate together. Sk8thing's real name is Shin. His moniker was coined by Fujiwara to distinguish "reptile shin" (Neighborhood's designer Shinsuke Takizawa, a reptile enthusiast) from "skate shin," which eventually evolved into Sk8thing. In 1988, Sk8thing, an avid illustrator, told Fujiwara that he wanted to start making T-shirts. Fujiwara took his first foray into clothing design very seriously and found apparel company backers, launching the first Ura-Hara brand, the skate-influenced GOODENOUGH,

Pages 186–189: Sk8thing remixed graphics from his various design work to create this layout especially for this book. Please enjoy!

in 1989. Former Plastics member and graphic designer Hajime Tachibana was drafted to teach the guys computer skills. When Nigo was ready to launch his own brand in 1992, he and Sk8thing created the direction of the brand together (Sk8thing came up with both the brand's name and its iconic logo graphic). In 1996, Sk8thing began work at Nigo's Nowhere office as a graphic designer, creating designs for all of his friend's brands, as he continues to do today for Neighborhood, Bounty Hunter, UNDER COVER, ELT, and Hectic, among others.

dev
gru
WANKERS
& THE CHOCOLATE FACTORY
DEVIOUS FUDGE
INTENSECURE Inc.
MFR: 94990 SER.NO.
CONTRACT: DAAB07-90-C-H025
US
THE GUILLOTINE
VOITKAMPF
ILLUMINATY
NEW
MENTAL FREE
mad coincidence!
BURGER WEAPON
GOTTI CIDER
Crook Gadget
MUSIC
THE BARRIER

Bounty Hunter was formed in 1995 by Hiraku Iwanaga and his business partner, Taka Suzuki. Opening initially in the Harajuku district of Tokyo, they would later extend their punk-and-paraphernalia formula to sister outlets in Osaka, Nagoya, and Fukuoka. Specializing in the iconography of short-run urban designs and hard-to-find collectibles from the 1970s, Bounty Hunter quickly generated a reputation as a cult boutique for customers seeking Sex Pistols, Ramones, or The Clash merchandise and *Star Wars*, Ultraman, or Cap'n Crunch commodities. Increasingly, they encouraged friends, colleagues, and fellow artists to contribute designs for their own lines of T-shirts. (One of these colleagues was the celebrated Japanese graphic designer Sk8thing.) While the brand designs and manufactures apparel, it is primarily considered a toy manufacturer, and has acted as one of the prime catalysts in the designer vinyl boom in Japan and the West.

Bounty Hunter decorates its clothing in black-and-white and bold graphical style. Shown here are graphics from the brands archives that feature the iconic skull, the looking-down-the-barrel-of-a-gun logo, and a homage to the Oakland Raiders football team logo.

SMART, RELAX & MINI
スマート、リラックス アンド ミニ

Japanese publisher Takarajima tapped into new subcultures with its eponymous magazine, followed by *CUTiE,* and in 1995 by *smart. smart* was dedicated to the burgeoning men's streetwear community that started forming in Harajuku's back streets with the opening of the shop Nowhere in 1993. *smart* helped to propel the underground community of dudes from neighborhood idols making silk-screened T-shirts into fashion celebrities with million-dollar brands. By the late 1990s, as part of a global streetwear trend and sneaker fever, Ura-Hara had become a part of mainstream commercialized culture. *smart*'s sister publication for a female readership, *mini,* was introduced in summer 2000. *mini* had a basic denim and T-shirt look and reported on Harajuku and the laid-back neighborhood Daikanyama. Its reign as the top girl trend magazine ended around 2003, when it could no longer compete with the popularity of Shibuya's *gyaru* culture, which was a switch from the young cute girl to a sexy girl—at least in affectation. Similarly, men's street casual culture also shifted from Ura-Hara to Daikanyama and Nakameguro. Although it had been around since 1996, Magazine House's *relax* magazine found its groove when it tapped into this new wave. The editorial teams injected elements of lifestyle and international (mostly street) art community into its formula with original artwork and covers by Mark Gonzales, Futura, Mike Mills, KAWS, and James Jarvis. It remained influential from 2000 to 2004, releasing its final issue in August 2006.

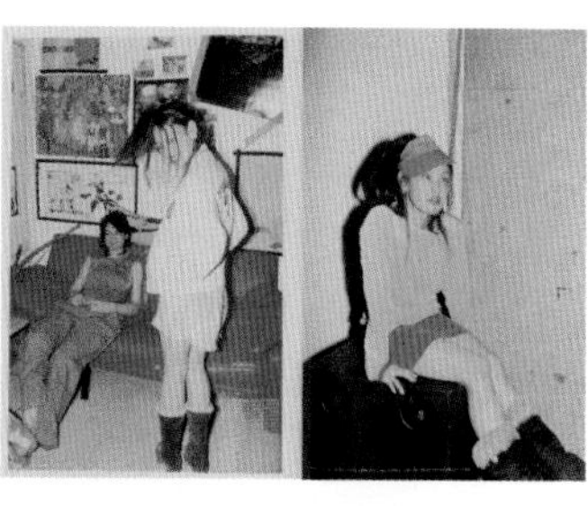

mart and its sister publication *mini* were the result of the ew, casual mainstream street fashion and culture that came ut of Ura-Hara in the 1990s. *smart* covers feature models, and designers, and celebrities, such as this October 2000 over featuring actor Tadanobu Asano (***opposite, top***). ***bove:*** March 2003 cover and interior image of *smart*. ***op:*** A March 2006 cover and interior spreads from *mini*, aturing its post-*CUTiE* tagline, "for NEW INDEPENDENT RLS." ***Opposite, bottom and this page:*** Striking cov- s for the streetwear lifestyle magazine *relax*'s September 00 issue by KAWS and September 2001 by Kate Gibbs.

X-GIRL エックスガール

From the low-key design of the logo by graphic artist Mike Mills to the casual snapshot catalogue images, X-girl embodies the laid-back Gen-X style of the '90s. Started in 1994 as the sister brand of the Beastie Boys' skater-influenced XLARGE®, X-girl also had musical roots in the form of one of its designers, ultracool rocker Kim Gordon of Sonic Youth. While the brand was not designed and manufactured in Japan, it quickly became embraced (along with Sofia Coppola's MILKFED), as the representative uniform of the new female streetwear movement in Tokyo. Channeling the vibes of the bubbling L.A. and New York cultural scenes, Gordon focused on designing outfits for the young urban girl. Basic miniskirts and T-shirts in vivid colors were street, girly, and fun—and represented a shift into post-*CUTiE* women's street fashion paralleled on the men's side by the new Ura-Hara styles. Both Gordon and Coppola had strong ties to the Japanese art and culture scenes. Their cool pedigrees and unfussy stylishness gave icon status to their brands, and gave young women a new stylistic model. In this, the labels were so wholeheartedly embraced by domestic girly street culture that they could almost be considered two of Harajuku's own.

While the Beastie Boys' Mike D was invo as an advisor to the men's streetwear bra XLARGE®, Kim Gordon served as co-de along with Daisy Von Furth of the sister b X-girl. The brand was known for its ultra and vintage inspired casual wear in bubb shades. The sensibility tapped into the ze and no doubt the small, form-fitting sizes to popularize the brand as well. Campaig images from the mid-1990s.

a-t-on
LO
HELLEY WINT
scénario de VLADIMIR N

ソフネット

SOPHNET.

A former employee at A.P.C., Hirofumi Kiyonaga started SOPHNET. with the A/W 1998 collection. From the very beginning, the brand had a chic style on a scale different from any other Harajuku label. The clothing is simple while having some hook to it, and hi-tech materials create a wholly unique urban style that is worn by a wide age range. Also, collections have featured the work of such popular artists as Julian Opie (opposite), Tatsuo Miyajima, and Jack Pierson. For A/W 1999, SOPHNET. and Nike released their first collection of their collaborative line, F.C.R.B. The concept of this line is an imaginary football (soccer) club. Along with a separate sports line, the phenomenal growth of this brand has influenced many major sport apparel companies. Neither brand is directed at a market of street teenagers; rather, the design and quality are meant for adults. This label can be considered the form of a matured "Harajuku culture." It also has a record label called "Music is Beautiful."

Opposite, top: An image from SOPHNET.'s S/S 2004 catalogue. Photograph by P.M. Ken. ***Opposite, inset:*** From the S/S 2005 collection, pieces decorated with art by Julian Opie. ***Opposite, left:*** Artwork for the S/S 2006 collection by Yoichi Takahashi featuring "Captain Tsubasa" from the well-known manga series of the same name, originally run in the 1980's edition of *Weekly Young Jump*. ***This page:*** *Hirofumi, fashion designer* is a portrait by Julian Opie of SOPHNET.'s designer Hirofumi Kiyonaga.

F.C.R.B.
エフシーアールビー

エフシーアールビー

Beginning in A/W 1999, Nike and SOPHNET. started designing a line of clothing called F.C.R.B. for the fictitious soccer team F.C.Real Bristol. P.M. Ken created the team's puppet-like members for the brand's catalogue. *Opposite:* A/W 2001/2002 catalogue. *Top:* S/S 2002 collection. *Above, right:* artwork for the S/S 2006 collection by Yoichi Takahashi featuring manga character "Captain Tsubasa." *Right:* F.C.Real Bristol on the field and ready to rumble for S/S 2007. *Left:* "After-practice" image from the S/S 2005 season.

VISVIM
ヴィズヴィム

Though it started in 2000 as a shoe brand, designer Hiroki Nakamura's Visvim has evolved into a more full-fledged label with a cult following. The brand examines the construction, materials, and design of timeless "products" such as military wear, chino pants, Chuck Taylor court shoes, American six-hole workboots, and Native American moccasins, re-engaging with designs that have seemed to reach a state of perfection but finding a way to add something new. Nakamura elevates this study of "the classics" to a science, as can be seen all the way down to the brand's logo—reminiscent of the periodic table of elements—and the dissertation-like, themed catalogues he releases each season. His shop F.I.L. (Free International Laboratory) expresses a cool but quirky sensibility, its gallery-style white space complemented by an abstract moose sculpture and live grass at the entrance (the installation reflects a trip Nakamura took to Alaska in his early twenties). A former designer at Burton Snowboards, Nakamura's unique sensibility is rooted in his firsthand experience with Native American cultures and their relationship to nature. The collections look basic, but it is in the details that Visvim scores points—streetwear in Egyptian cotton and cashmere, chino pants with military detailing, and outerwear with a 3-D industrial design flair. The shoes are hybrids that fuse high-tech sneaker materials and design with an outdoor sensibility and references to Native American moccasins. Their construction, including hand-sewn detailing and subtly luxurious pigskin linings, reveal Nakamura's true *otaku* obsessive style.

Nakamura H.

VISVIM FW06-07

Dissertation on Animal Mechanics
Design of Product Versus Nature of Performance

from:
The Free International Laboratory
(TOKYO, JAPAN : 2006)

CUBISM
F.I.L.

©Copyright 2001 Cubism Inc
Trademark of visvim licensed by Cubism Inc.

visvim

This page, top: Visvim's Harajuku boutique is located on a back street not far from the Christian Dior boutique and Kiddy Land. With a Spartan's sense of décor, the concrete walls painted white, and exposed ceiling rings are more reminiscent of Belgian designer Martin Margiela than Ura-Hara. *Opposite and below:* F/W 06 catalogue was given the title "Dissertation on Animal Mechanics. Design of Product Versus Nature of Performance." The catalog is illustrated with a moose sculpture (which is on display at the Tokyo boutique), the quilted Polke shoe that has pigskin lining, the moccasin/running shoe fusion The FBT, and Visvim's take on the classic M65 and military topcoat merged with outdoor Gore-Tex technology.

We Love You, Vivienne

ウィーラヴユー、ヴィヴィアン

By Keiko Hirayama

Since the second half of the 1960s, Harajuku has been highly attuned to trends in fashion, and is now recognized as the birthplace of Japanese street fashion. In the '60s, young people would rent a room in an apartment building in the neighborhood, move in with a sewing machine (and little else), and design their own clothing. Being fashion conscious, they loved foreign clothing, and from the early times of Swinging London they walked around Harajuku with a pop fashion style—colorful sweaters and socks, with weird sunglasses. They have always been drawn to London fashion, but what they really loved, a style that took hold at the same time as the first wave of Harajuku designers, was the punk aesthetic of Vivienne Westwood.

The punk style began in 1976 when Westwood and her collaborator Malcolm McLaren mixed several elements of pop culture into clothes with an anarchic, rebellious spirit that was carried along in the cultural revolution embodied by the Sex Pistols and other bands that swept across international youth culture. While in England punk was a rebellion against a closed society (among other things), in Japan the message of "anarchy" was conveyed significantly as a form of fashion, while the music also challenged Japan's old moral and value systems.

In 1982, Westwood announced that she was "tired of being underground," and started showing in Paris collections. Because she got her start on the streets—not in the establishment *maisons* of Paris—Japanese designers felt an allegiance to her and her outsider status. In 1989, former Westwood model Hisako Nakagawa organized the *Vivienne Westwood Fashion Show* at Tokyo's Spiral Hall, just a few minutes' walk from the east end of Harajuku's Omotesando. From 2,000 items of Westwood's clothes collected by Japanese fans (hole-gutted punk T-shirts, bondage suits, mohair sweaters, pirate shirts . . .), one hundred sixty were selected and modeled by their owners for the show. Westwood said, "I was surprised to find out how much the Japanese have collected my clothing."

The excitement of the exhibition hall demonstrated just how passionately people felt about Westwood's clothing, and, in 1994, inspired me as a curator to hold the *Punk* exhibition at Shiseido's Art Space in Ginza. There was a strong interest among young people for her work. Westwood is a kindred spirit of Comme des Garçons' Rei Kawakubo and UNDER COVER's Jun Takahashi, and the Ura-Hara men's shops were already exhibiting a punk attitude. And Westwood's revolutionary mix of traditional and historical English fashion elements—tartan check, Victorian cuffs, corsets, bustle, crinoline—have a sense of costume play evident today in Japanese fashion's Goth-Loli style (whose adherents also like her iconic wedges and high-heel shoes).

There is music, immediacy, and a sense of life to her fashion. And it is cool. The punk element helped Harajuku kids identify fashion as a subculture that could allow them to express their own social allegiances and grievances. Japanese street fashion picked up those elements freely and remixed them in a unique manner (at times disjointed from their original meanings, but still keeping the original spirit.)

irts designed by Vivienne Westwood and Malcolm
:Laren in 1976 for their Seditionaries collection.
a-Hara designers aggressively amassed as many of
se T-shirts as possible. Other influential Westwood-
Laren collections include Teddy Boy inspired Let
Rock (1970), the rocker themed Too Fast To Live,
Young To Die (1972), and fetish wear Sex (1974).
stwood's first independent collection, the S/S 1985
ni-Crini, incorporated crinoline and lace and rocking
se platform shoes. These elements were flirtatious
d became hugely popular in Harajuku, setting the tone
the look of many. Masayuki Yoshinaga's street snaps
he late 1990s, shown here, reveal the prevalence
Westwood's influence, which was the segue for
ajuku's Lolita movement.

UNDER COVER
アンダーカバー

Jun Takahashi (also known as Jonio) is the designer, owner, and director of the brand UNDER COVER. The brand got its start in the late 1990s, a time when other brands would coalesce as the Ura-Hara movement. Since then the brand has grown in scope, moving through styles and genres with frenetic speed. Nonetheless, the brand can be relied upon for dark, heavy clothing with bizarre graphics straight out of a nightmare and detailed finishing that would be found on a doll's outfit. The brand's early focus on Tokyo men's street fashion was certainly no indication of the women's runway fashion Jonio would show in Paris years later.

In high school, Jonio took the train from the countryside into Harajuku to go to A Store Robot, the first shop to carry Vivienne Westwood's Seditionaries line in Japan. Jonio was eager to make punk clothes and went to fashion school at Bunka Fashion College in Shinjuku. He started silk-screening T-shirts using the name UNDER COVER before finishing school in 1990. Hip-hop and DJ culture were then emerging in Japan. All the fashion students either had a band or played music, and flocked to popular clubs. Jonio was in a Sex Pistols cover band in the early 1990s; his friend Nigo occasionally sat in on drums. Milk's Hitomi Okawa took Jonio and Nigo around to the clubs and introduced the good friends to the editor-in-chief of *Takarajima* as being the coolest kids around. Beginning with *Takarajima*, numerous magazines offered them regular columns to feature an A-to-Z of their favorite things of the moment. Jonio and Nigo's joint column, "LastOrgy2," started in 1993 and was so popular that the men's street magazines *Asayan* and *smart* also ran their columns, titled "LastOrgy3" and "4-LOM," respectively. The columns helped make them celebrities, and gave them a platform to introduce brands and goods that they liked (often stuff made by their friends), and later to promote their own store and brands.

With Okawa introducing Jonio to the fashion world, the pair went to a Comme des Garçons show, in which Jonio saw pure punk (the price tags were also a shock). He decided to become serious about fashion, but high rather than street fashion. Seeing Martin Margiela's mind-blowing clothes for the first time was also a pivotal moment. Here were fashions that looked like his own, selling in a major department store for serious yen. He traces this as the inspiration for his focus on women's clothing, unusual given the Ura-Hara scene's focus on men's street- and sportswear. He began selling his clothes at Okawa's Milk shop just before he and Nigo opened their shop, Nowhere, in 1993.

Jonio's fashions take a characteristically Japanese, more conceptual approach to clothes than that of Western designers, even while he may take inspiration from Western styles. The question seems to be how to make a garment in a way that has never been considered. As the name implies, UNDER COVER designs take a subversive approach, communicating an aesthetic through music and staging and props rather than emphasizing garment design.

Traveling in much the same direction as his friend and Nowhere colleague Nigo, Jonio has been shifting gears from being underground to working toward broader brand recognition. His first Paris collection showed in 2002, and there are now more than seventy shops that sell UNDER COVER abroad, including L'Eclaireur in Paris and Barneys New York. While the UNDER COVER brand has moved beyond its Ura-Hara focus and roots, it has retained a punk sensibility throughout the many phases of its development. Collections titled Scab, Languid, or But Beautiful . . . sound like teen-angst-inspired albums, but also point to Jonio's dark visual poetry.

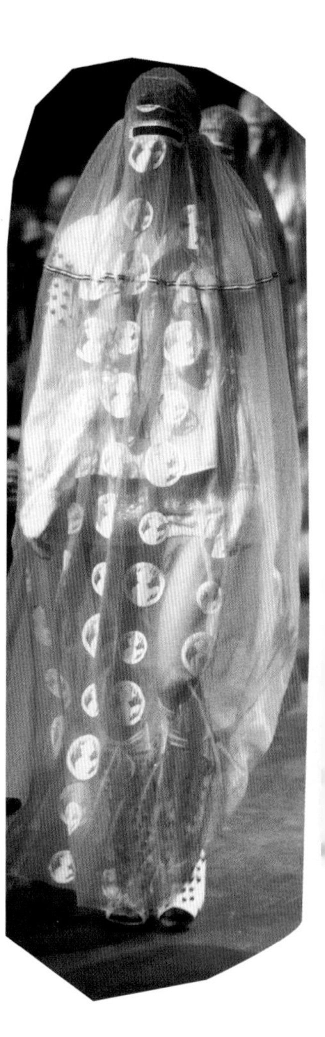

Pages 204–205: Images from UNDER COVER's S/S 2004 collection Languid (also *opposite, bottom right.*) *Opposite left and center:* The A/W 2004 Paper Doll collection. *This page:* After eight years of showing in Tokyo, the S/S 2003 collection SCAB was the UNDER COVER's Paris debut collection.

Opposite: A/W 2005's But Beautiful . . . was inspired by artist Anne Valérie Dupont, who taught Jonio how to make dolls. ***This page, left and center:*** S/S 2005 But Beautiful II, an homage to Czech filmmaker Jan Švankmajer, once again puzzled the Paris crowd. Takahashi entrusts the hair and makeup of his shows to Katsuya Kamo. ***This page, right:*** The finale of rocker boy inspired A/W 2006 Arts & Crafts.

Jun Takahashi is the essence of Japanese cool, from his hanging curtain of hair to his black boots with tiny silver spoons tied to the laces.
—Suzy Menkes

Opposite, left: The S/S 2006 T. collection was based on an imaginary progressive-rock band from Germany. Its candle-filled presentation was a moody extravaganza. *Opposite, center and right:* A/W 2007 BBV Guruguru was a collection of models covered head-to-toe, causing some controversy among journalists. *This page:* Takahashi makes a 180-degree turn of aesthetics. Inspired by his experiences in Paris, the designer simplifies the ideal of the UNDER COVER woman, making her classically beautiful in this S/S 2007 collection. The show's soundtrack, an acoustic version of PIL's "This is Not a Love Song," nods to her dark, punk roots.

Re:Re: mojojo

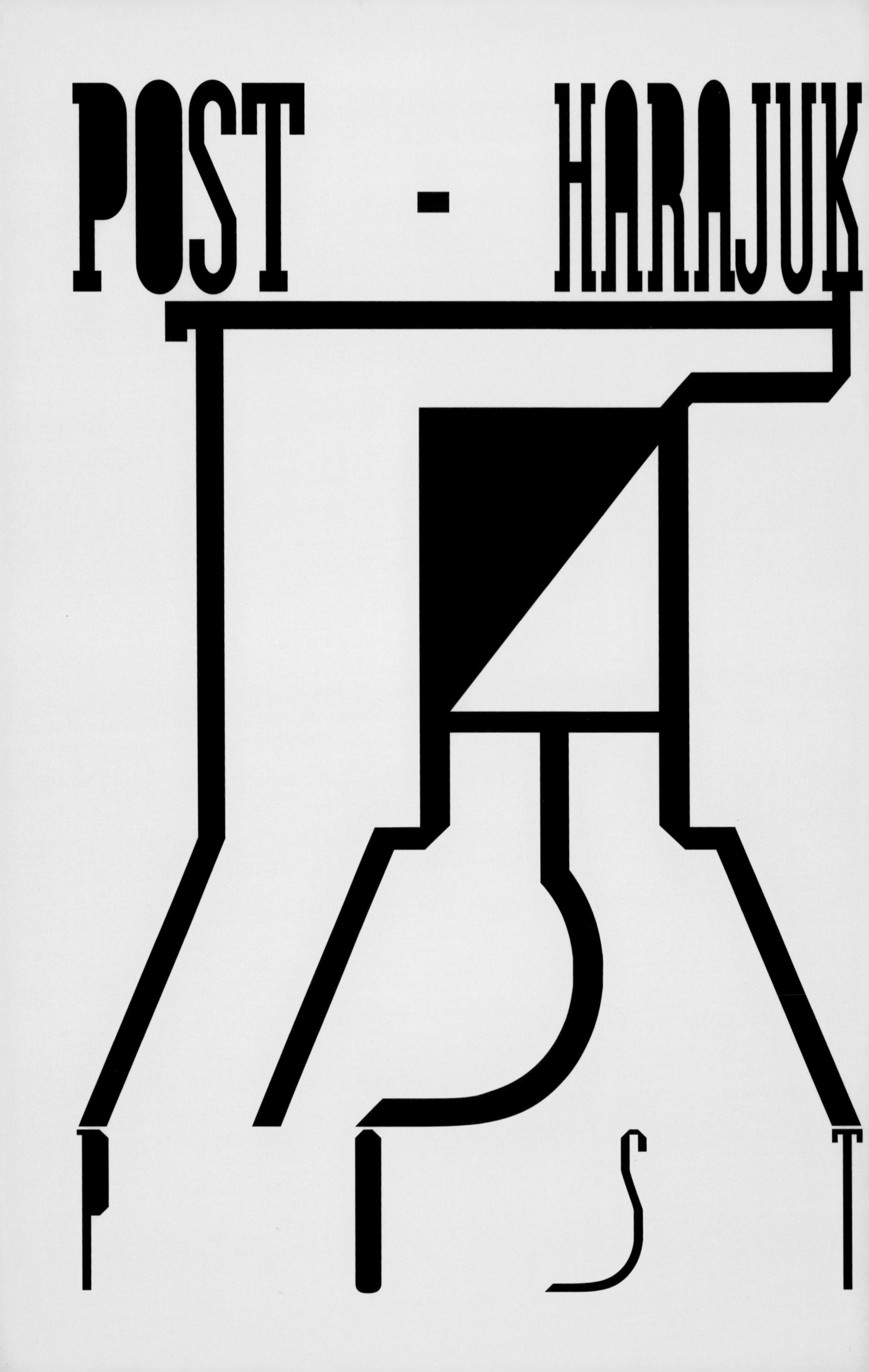
POST - HARAJUK
POST

I don't want to go to heaven—I want to be a Harajuku girl! Japan is one of the most amazing places and cultures I have ever been to, and every time I go, I want to go again. The Harajuku district is one of my favorite places to explore; kitsch over culture, presented with such a cartoonlike, childlike glee that it has as much of a sugar rush as being shut in a candy store. It is colorful, curious, a blur between reality and fairytale, and where all good Galliano girls go.
—John Galliano

THE FUTURE OF HARAJUKU

Young Dreams and Happy Chaos

by Takeji Hirakawa

After the bubble economy burst in the mid-1990s, the generation of Japanese now in their twenties and thirties has only a dim memory of a time before the phenomenal economic growth and livelihood that carries on in Japan's consumer culture. There is a pervading sense that Japan's hyper-consumerist climate has hobbled any salient cultural sense of self for Japanese young people, and that there is a growing alienation among young people. We see glimpses of this in the Tokyo depicted in Yasuo Tanaka's 1981 novel *Nantonaku Kurisutaru,* in Takashi Homma's photography series *Tokyo Suburbia,* and in the music of Shibuya's Cornelius—a curious complacency, and an acceptance of deep disconnection. This is the era of the "affluent refugees," who relish the new and can readily buy what they want. Ready and easy access to part-time work and the concurrent expansion of the service industry in Japan has meant that young people have their own money and don't have to rely on their parents to

There is a pervading sense that Japan's hyper-consumerist climate has hobbled any salient cultural sense of self for Japanese young people, and that there is a growing alienation among young people.

彼らたちの心の奥にはいつしか、ある共通した疎外感や不安感そして、アパシーな心のあり様を満ち足りない何かを「寂しさ」として感じ始めた世代でも在る。この次元から彼ら達を読むと、彼らたち以降の日本人たちは、「寂しい個人主義」を背負い込んでしまった国民とも言える。

Nozomi Ishiguro started his eponymous line in 1998. The former Junya Watanabe Comme des Garçons assistant's fashions are favored by the Harajuku avant-garde. 2007 S/S collection at Kabuki-cho, Shinjuku.

Shima hair was first a rage in the 1990s. The salon chain's second coming is thanks to Nara Yuya (center) who joined the Harajuku branch. This "charisma hairstylist" is one of Harajuku's fashion icons.

そして、いつの間にかそれらは、外国モノ・コピー思考から日本発の日本モノ指向へと、ある種の彼らたちの恵まれた消費環境が自信を与え、価値観をも変えていきはじめる。

make personal purchases. Undoubtedly, this generation has a new independence, regardless of their maturity levels. We can only speculate what will be the outcome. The Harajuku designers featured in this book have all exhibited a D.I.Y. spirit and entrepreneurial gumption that is encouraging—the opposite of complacency—as well as leadership qualities, individuality, creativity, and a sense of exploration, while being connected. But their success hinges in part on the new consumer culture.

Shopping culture, which remained firmly in place among Japanese youth even after the bubble burst, helped drive the demand for street fashion, and the innovative streetwear of Harajuku in particular. The mid-1980s saw an

There was a switch from copying the West to creating original Japanese items, a wa-mono *(made-in-Japan) boom. Japanese kids were co-opting foreign styles and creating their own particularly Japanese street culture.*

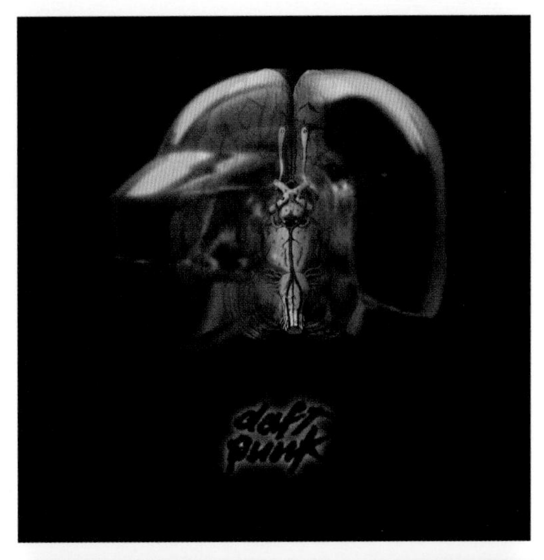

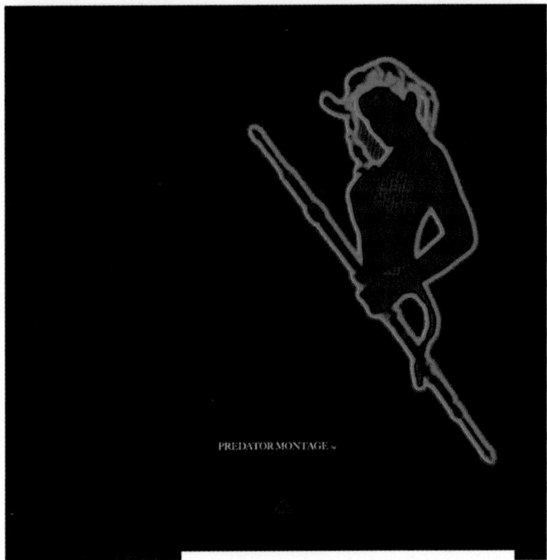

NEXUSVII's menswear is in the Ura-Hara tradition, but designer Tomohiro Konno (only in his late 20s) has found his own footing, already designing for Stüssy and for artist KAWS' brand Original Fake. ***Above:*** NEXUSVII T-shirt graphics.

Regardless of the commercialization, copycat culture, and other less-than-desirable factors that have all become part of Harajuku's now well-structured and established consumer society, for young designers, coming there to create and show their work is the first step toward realizing a dream of success in the world of Japanese fashion.

explosion of Japanese pop, hip-hop, punk, and dance music that was highly visual and coincided with the impulses of street fashion, establishing a new, clearly formed youth culture in Tokyo. There were Japanese designers, Japanese stores, Japanese magazines, an entire Japanese market. There was a switch from copying the West to creating original Japanese items, a *wa-mono* (made-in-Japan) boom. Japanese kids were co-opting foreign styles and creating their own particularly Japanese street culture. This can also be seen as a newfound confidence among young Japanese creators fostered by the rich consumer environment.

In Harajuku, which has come to be shorthand for street fashion culture, there is the "street reality" of what's actually being worn and why, and an idealization of what the neighborhood represents. Regardless of the commercialization, copycat culture, and other less-than-desirable factors that have all become part of Harajuku's now well-structured and established consumer society, for young designers, coming there to create and show their work is the first step toward realizing a dream of success in the world of Japanese fashion. And for the kids shopping in the neighborhood, its energy and history offer the potential for personal style and expression. "Harajuku" is not just a physical location, it is a symbolic environment for those who want to do (or be) something new.

Harajuku itself is a medium through which information is transferred. Dressing up and being seen on the streets of Harajuku is a form of communication, another bit of data in a stream of exchange, articulated through the street fashion photographs taken there for magazines past and present, such as *mc Sister, Zipper, Fine, CUTiE, FRUiTS,* and the street-snap magazines that followed.

But there is a threat to Harajuku's livelihood as a focus of creative, bottom-up, street-level fashion energy: soaring real estate values. In the early '80s, one *tsubo* (about 3.3 square meters) used to cost between 25,000

Faline is a colorful, closet-sized boutique off of Takeshita-dori, owned and operated by international party girl extraordinaire Baby Mary (center). Much like Milk, this is a gathering spot for the next generation of kids.

and 30,000 yen (between $200 and $250 at current exchange rates) per month to rent. It will soon cost three times that amount. The businesses that can afford such rates—"adult" and international brands with considerable financial capital such as the Gap, Chanel, Louis Vuitton, Prada, Chloé, Tod's, Ralph Lauren, Nike, and Adidas—have built new fashion-institution buildings there, capitalizing on and buying a bit of the "Harajuku magic" while helping price out the sort of independent, truly street-level young creators who put the neighborhood on the map. Doujunkai, a row of low-rise brick apartment buildings—home to many artists and small shops and galleries for years—was torn down to build Omotesando Hills, a collection of luxury boutiques that opened in 2006. The locality of the neighborhood is giving way to a creeping sameness, with the same brands available here as anywhere else. Even off the high profile store-lined dragstrip of Omotesando, this has also become true in Ura-Hara, Harajuku's back streets. Accordingly, new labels such as Device (started and based in Kyoto), the shop Faline (based in Nagoya), and conglomerate-owned Cannabis (based in Ueno) are all enterprises originally built up by owners who don't hail from Harajuku. New brands launching in the district, like NEXUSVII, W-Taps, and Visvim (which also now has its own shop), are considered post–Ura-Hara brands. There is also Mister Hollywood, DOG (a secondhand store), WJK, and #44.

But for the kids who dream of a life in fashion, and through fashion, Harajuku still offers an image. It is a dream, an identity, a launching pad, a business model, and a happy chaos.

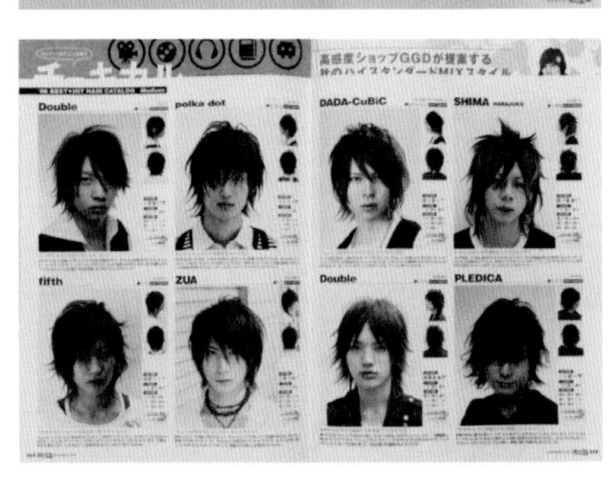

Choki Choki is a magazine that presents a catalog guide to the hottest hair and fashion trends for highly style-obsessed teens and 20-something guys. Contents revolve around "Oshyare Kings" (kings of cool) who aren't professional models per se, but rather personalities that have some charisma or presence.

Spank!, Spank Me!, and Chelsea are stores located in the outskirts of Harajuku operated for and by kids born in the 1980s. Bubble gum pink D.I.Y. rock T-shirts, inspired by 1980s rocker chic Niki Corvette and the Care Bears, hang next to vintage finds. As their motto goes: "So Cute!! Hug me! Love me! Spank me!"

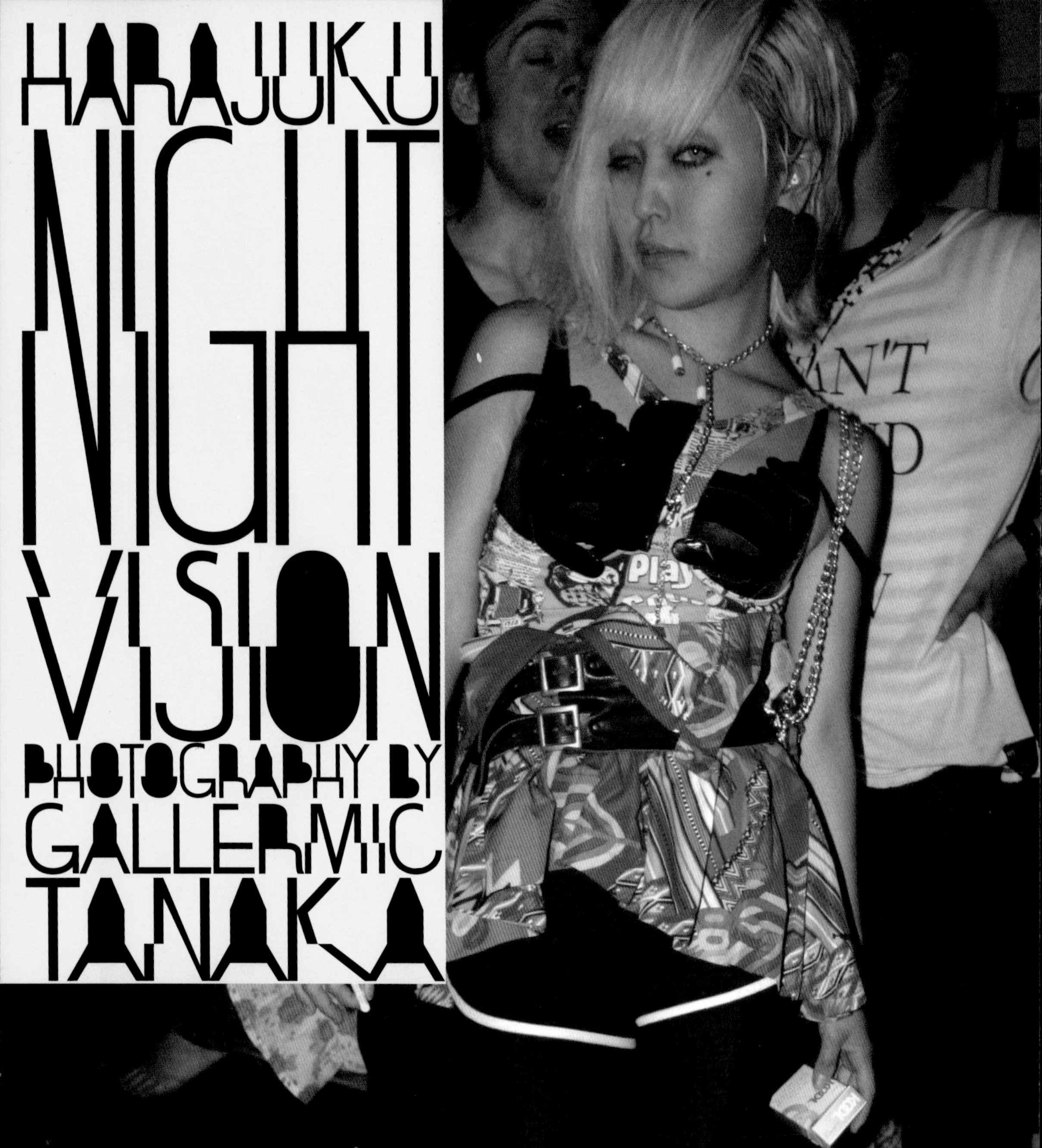
HARAJUKU
NIGHT
VISION
PHOTOGRAPHY BY
GALLERMIC
TANAKA

LONDON

Pinky-D
Pinky-D
SPANK! RECORD
SPANK! RECORD

SEX
SEX
SEX

Symbols

A

B

C

D

E

F

G

H

I

J

K

L

M

N

O

TIFFANY GODOY

Tiffany Godoy has lived in Japan since 1997, when she began working as a fashion editor for the Japanese culture magazine *Composite* and then subsequently for *Studio Voice*. She is a contributing editor and writer for *Vogue Nippon*, *V Magazine*, the *New York Times Magazine*, *Self Service*, *WWD*, and *Interview*. She has served as a creative consultant for fashion and advertising companies in Japan, and, along with Tomoyuki Yonezu, makes up the art direction unit Erotyka.

MARIKO SUZUKI

Since the early 1990s, Mariko Suzuki has been tracking the cool kids on the streets of Harajuku. In 1997 she joined the editorial team of *KERA*, where she served as editor-in-chief until the its 57th issue, during which time it became the barometer for Goth-Loli kids. In December 2000, she started the magazine *Gothic & Lolita Bible*, serving as its editor-in-chief until the 8th. issue. Suzuki is currently the editor-in-chief of *KERA Maniax*.

KEIKO HIRAYAMA

Keiko Hirayama is a freelance writer and fashion director involved with the planning and launching of new brands. She started out in the advertising department of the cosmetics company Shiseido and eventually served as the editor-in-chief of Shiseido's trade publication *Hanatsubaki* from 1982 to 1992. She was also the organizer of Shiseido's fashion events and art exhibitions. She is the author of *The Paris Collection: 51 Designers*.

TOMOYUKI YONEZU

After establishing the design office Enlightenment, Tomoyuki Yonezu's commercial and personal work has drawn a lot of attention. Along with fashion editor Tiffany Godoy, he is part of the art direction team Erotyka. He is also active independently as an art director and graphic designer for the fashion, music, and advertising industries.

IVAN VARTANIAN

Ivan Vartanian is the director of Goliga Books, Inc., based in Tokyo. His publications include *Egon Schiele: Drawings and Watercolors* (Thames & Hudson, 2000), *Drop Dead Cute: The New Generation of Women Artists in Japan* (Chronicle Books, 2001), *Setting Sun: Writings by Japanese Photographers* (Aperture, 2005), *Full Vinyl: The Subversive Art of Designer Toys* (Collins Design, 2006), among other publications.

TETSUYA SUZUKI

Tetsuya Suzuki was involved in the influential Tokyo men's street fashion magazine *smart* since its inception in 1995. He then founded and served as editor-in-chief of the men's magazine *smart Max*. Since 2004, he has worked as an independent writer and editor focusing on Tokyo's street scene. In 2005, he and Hiroshi Fujiwara launched the lifestyle, fashion, and music web magazine *honeyee.com* and currently serves as its editor-in-chief.

TAKEJI HIRAKAWA

Hirakawa is a professor of fashion, freelance journalist, and a frequent contributor to *W.W.D. Japan*, and *Nippon Seni Shinbun*. Currently he lectures on fashion as a guest professor at the Kyoto University of Art and Design. He has also served on the jury of numerous fashion colleges and fashion contests. From 2002 to 2004, he organized an annual exhibition "Discipline-JAP" at Antwerp's Incubation Gallery.

MAKOTO SEKIKAWA

Makoto Sekikawa was the editor-in-chief of *Takajima* magazine from 1980 to 1989, and the founding editor-in-chief of *CUTiE*, editing the magazine from 1989 to 1994. Since then he has served as the chief director of Takarajima publishing's fashion titles.

ACKNOWLEDGMENTS

This book would not been possible without the love and encouragement of mom, dad, grandma, Courtney, and Vanessa. Thank you for always believing in me. Thank you to Ivan Vartanian for his faith in me and generosity. You are my brother. Masa Sugatsuke, Hiroyuki Kato, and Yuko Birukawa and Femme for giving me a chance. Tomoyuki Yonezu, Kaoru Inoue, Roko Mishima, Masa Kanazawa for the love you have given this crazy gaijin girl for so many years.

Thank you to everyone who so generously gave their time and shared their inspiring stories, making the process of doing research such a fun adventure. Thanks to Kaz Yamamuro and Yoshikazu Katagiri of INFAS Publications, Ai Mitsuda and Yohji Yamamoto, Art Bird Books, Asuka Eito, Mana Igarashi, Hirofumi Kurino and United Arrows, Katsumi Yamada, Goro and Mito Yamamoto, Ruki Matsumo and Ba-tsu, Teru and Takashi and the AG crew, Mariko Nishitani and Bunka, Howard Lichter, Fumihiro Hayashi, Hiroshi Isobe, Motoi Itoh, Kiddy Land, Andrew Bunney at Gimme 5, Jelka Music, Shauna Toohey of P.A.M., Tim Clifton-Green and Vivienne Westwood, Griffin, JJ Farrer, and the ladies of Jimmy Choo. A very special thanks to Shizuyo Kusunoki.

Thank you to all of the designers, photographers, stylists, hair and make-up artists, models, publishing houses, and artists who have contributed to this book. You are a true inspiration. Vive made in Japan.

Kumiko Takano and Across, Hiroshi Hakamori, Naoki Sakai, Yasuhiro Hamano, Takeji Hirakawa, Yacco, Masayoshi Sukita, David Bowie, Iggy Pop, Saburo Tatsuki, Yuri Kaneko, Isao Kaneko, Masateru Uehara, Nobuyo Fujikura, Haruka Nagamori, Shigeki Nakazato and Magazine House, INFAS Publications, Bishin Jumonji, Tadanori Yokoo, Ikko Tanaka, Iman, Michiyo Tanabe and Takeo Kikuchi, Shoji Ueda, Nobushige Tanino and World, Hitomi Okawa, Shingo Yasuda and Milk, Ryota Atsumi, Hinano and Mune, Yama-chan and Cream Soda, Hiroshi Morinaga, Mayumi Miwa, Yuko Nakamura, Kaoru Ijima, Toshi Nakanishi, Chica Sato and The Plastics,Yama-chan and Saito-san and Ozone Community, Maripol, Chigako Takeda, Keiko Mimoto and Comme des Garçons, Makoto Sekikawa, Hiroko Nukitani, Sijiro Sato, Chisako Minoura and Takarajimasha, Miwako Ichikawa, Laforet, Nagi Noda, Takuya Onuki, Nobu Kitamura and Hysteric Glamour, Takashi Homma, Rowland Kirishima, Terry Richardson, Moriyama Daido, Patti Smith, Sonya Park, Higashi Ishida and Aloha State, Sayaka Yoshino, Katsuya Kamo and Mod's Hair, Hiromix, Shinbiyo, Libération, Olivier Zahm and Purple Fashion, Aya Tanizaki, Sachi, Kae, Anna Kanehara, Super Lovers, Shoichi Aoki and Rei Shito of Lens Co., Ltd., Masahiro Saito and Fötus, Lika Azechi and Masahiro Nakagawa of 20471120, Masaki Matsuhima, Satoshi Saikusa and Mika Mizutani, Jean-Baptiste Mondino, Takao Yamashita and beauty: beast, Keiko and Christopher Nemeth, Mark Lebon, *i-D* magazine, Masayuki Yoshinaga and Media Factory, Mariko Suzuki and Index Communications, h. NAOTO, Muga Miyahara, Takahiro Sakuma, Fumiyo Isobe and Baby, The Stars Shine Bright, Raine, TBS, SEX POT ReVeNGE, Makoto Ueda, Trashlight Vision, Susumu Miyawaki, Antique Café, Megu, Kai Regan, Mana and Midi Nette, Tetsuya Suzuki, Hiroshi Fujiwara, *HUGE*, Yasuhiro Hamazaki, Nigo and A Bathing Ape, Nylon guys, Marvin Scott Jarrett, Sanrio, Def Jam, Sk8thing, Bounty Hunter, KAWS, Kate Gibbs, X-girl, Hirofumi Kiyonaga and SOPHNET., F.C.R.B., P.M. Ken, Yoichi Takahashi, Julian Opie, Hiroki Nakamura and Visvim, Masakazu Kunitake, Jun Takahashi and UNDER COVER, Nozomi Ishiguro, Shima, NEXUSVII, Baby Mary and the Faline girls, Gallermic Tanaka and the Harajuku kids. Special thanks to Ayumi Tanabe and her agency Energy for allowing her image to be used as the book's cover.

Thank you to Stephen Jones, Gene Krell, Shu Uemura, Patricia Field, David Byrne, Edison Chen, Michael Koppleman, Shawn Stussy, and John Galliano who were so kind to share their thoughts and words about Harajuku.

My long-time collaborator Tomoyuki Yonezu gave the book its beautiful form, making peace amongst all the different styles and general chaos that is Harajuku. We were also gifted with a talented and dedicated team of industrious designers who help execute the ardous task of design and layout. Thank you Mariko Kobori, Yasuhito Takeuchi, Miyuki Hentona, and Naoto Kimura.

Along with my editor, Ivan Vartanian, we would like to give thanks to the following individuals who have generously contributed their time, efforts, careful attention, as well as good humor and encouragement despite the demands of their schedules: Akiko Iizuka, Yumiko Yata, Kyoko Wada, Asako Nambu, Kumiko Masuya, and Takuya Uchiyama. Thank you to William Campbell, Valerie Koehn, and Lester T. L. Fykes, Jr. for reading through the book and catching all the typos. Thank you to David Marx and John Storey for reading the manuscript and providing valuable commentary. Thank you to Brett MacFadden of Chronicle Books. Steve Mockus, also of Chronicle Books, was an invaluable member to our team, helping to rein in the manuscript and shepherding the book to completion. Rico Komanoya helped keep the show running and was always ready with a smile. A gold star to Eric A. Clauson for his continued support.

ILLUSTRATION CREDITS

Unless otherwise indicated all work appears with the permission and courtesy of the contributor. All artwork, photography, illustration, design, brand names, and typography is protected by copyright laws and conventions. All secondary rights are retained by the contributors.

PH = Photographer, M = Model, AD = Art Director, CD = Creative Director, D = Designer, ST = Stylist, H = Hair Stylist, MU = Make-up Artist

Front cover: *Clutch* advertising 1996 PH Higashi Ishida, ST Sonya Park, H&MU Katsuya Kamo, M Ayumi Tanabe. **Page 14 top left:** PH Hiroshi Hakamori (Parco Co., Ltd); **top right:** courtesy of Jun; **middle right:** courtesy of HAMANO INSTITUTE; **bottom left and right:** www.web-across.com (Parco Co., Ltd.). **Page 16 top left and bottom:** www.web-across.com (Parco Co., Ltd.); **top right:** PH Hiroshi Hakamori (Parco Co., Ltd.). **Page 25:** PH Masayoshi Sukita. **Pages 26–27:** PH copyright Shoji Ueda Office. **Page 28 top:** *An An* (Magazine House, Ltd.) March 20 1970 No. 1, PH Saburo Tatsuki; **middle:** June 5 1971 No. 32, PH Saburo Tatsuki, M Yuri Tachikawa, H Masako Matsumura; **bottom:** June 5 1971 No. 32, PH Saburo Tatsuki, Clothing by Mitsuhiro Matsuda, M Yuri Tachikawa. **Page 29:** June 5 1970 No. 6, PH Saburo Tatsuki, Clothing by Isao Kaneko, M Yuri Tachikawa. **Page 30 top left:** March 20 1970 No. 1, PH Saburo Tatsuki, Clothing by Isao Ito, H Masako Matsumura, M Yuri Tachikawa; **middle:** December 20 1970 No. 19, PH Saburo Tatsuki, Clothing by Isao Kaneko, H Masako Matsumura, M Yuri Tachikawa; **bottom:** June 20 1971 No. 31, PH Saburo Tatsuki, Clothing by Masami Aramaki, H Hiro Ishida, M Hideo Saito. **Page 31 top right:** July 20 1970 No. 9, PH Saburo Tatsuki, H Masako Matsumura, M Yuri Tachikawa, Vero; **bottom right:** November 5 1970 No. 16, PH Saburo Tatsuki, H Masako Matsumura, M Hideo Saito, Hani Rainu, D Ayumi Ohashi; **left:** April 5 1970 No. 2, PH Saburo Tatsuki, Clothing by Isao Kaneko, M Yuri Tachikawa. **Page 34:** *Ryuko-Tsushin* (INFAS Publications); **top:** June 1980 No. 197, AD Tadanori Yokoo, PH Taiji Arita, H&MU Yasuo Nagaya; **bottom:** April 1980 No. 195 AD Tadanori Yokoo PH Bishin Jumonji. **Page 35:** January 1978 No. 167, AD Ikko Tanaka, PH Noriaki Yokosuka, M Iman. **Page 38 top:** *Milk Bar* magazine Summer 1998, No. 5 PH Milk; **bottom:** *Milk Bar* magazine, Spring 2001, No. 8, PH Ryota Atsumi, M Hinano Yoshikawa, Mune from the band Spica. **Page 44–49:** *Harajuku UFO* Yuko Nakamura (Canal Co., Ltd.), January 1980. **Pages 50, 52–53:** PH Kaoru Ijima. **Page 52:** Artwork Toshio Nakanishi. **Page 54–55:** PH Maripol. **Pages 56, 58–63:** PH courtesy of Comme des Garçons. **Pages 58–59 bottom left:** *Six* (Comme des Garçons Co., Ltd.) 1988 No.1 and "COMME des GARÇONS Noir", PH Sachiko Kuru. **Page 60 top:** PH Masayuki Hayashi. **Page 69:** *CUTiE* (Takarajima Publishing) June 1 1994, PH Yoshihiro Kawaguchi ST Sonya Park, H&MU Ryoji Inagaki, M Miwako Ichikawa. **Page 70:** October 14 1996, PH Kazunari Tajima, ST Sonya Park, H&MU Hiromi Kobari, M Hinano Yoshikawa. **Page 71 top:** October 1 1995, PH Ryu Tamagawa, ST Kyoko Fushimi, H Kenjiro Akama, MU Naomi Kubota, M Miwako Ichikawa; **bottom:** October 1 1994, PH Kazunari Tajima, ST Sonya Park, H&MU Ryoji Inagaki, M Miwako Ichikawa. **Page 72:** January 17 No. 166, PH Kishin Shinoyama, H&MU Katsuko Hasegawa, M Rin Kozue, Yoppy, Hikaru. **Page 73 top:** October 1 1993 No. 48, PH Yasuo Matsumoto, ST Mie Hataki, M Miwako Ichikawa; **bottom left:** October 1 1995 No. 72, PH Ryu Tamagawa, Keisuke Naito, Hiroshi Sugawara, Yoshiyuki Ugazin; **bottom right:** October 1 1995 No. 63. **Page 74:** October 11 2003 No. 243, PH Keisuke Nagase, ST Miho Kobayashi, M Uki. **Page 75:** October 12 2004 No. 255, PH Junji Ishiguro, ST Shino Suganuma, H&MU Noboru Tomizawa, M Chiaki Kuriyama. **Pages 76–81:** Courtesy and copyright Laforet Harajuku Co., Ltd, advertising Spring 2001, AD Nagi Noda, D Mitsuyo Sakuma, PH Shoji Uchida, ST Kyoko Fushimi, H Shinya, MU Coco, Flower art by Musubi Aoki. **Page 78 top and middle:** Laforet advertising Fall, and Winter 1998, AD Takuya Onuki, D Taro Terada, Yasuto Arai, Katsuhiro Shimizu, PH Shintaro Shiratori; **bottom:** Laforet advertising Renewal 2001, AD/CD Takuya Onuki, D Sachihiro Kawada, PH Moto Matsumoto Motography. **Page 79:** Laforet advertising Fall 1997, AD Takuya Onuki, D Taro Terada, Yasuto Arai, Katsuhiro Shimizu, PH Shintaro Shiratori. **Page 81 top:** Laforet advertising Winter 1995, AD/CD Takuya Onuki, D Takuya Onuki, Kazuhiro Kishi, PH Shintaro Shiratori; **bottom:** Laforet advertising 2001, AD Takuya Onuki, D Sachihiro Kawada, PH Takeshi Kanou. **Page 82:** Laforet commercial Christmas 2004, AD Nagi Noda, FD Nagi Noda, CA Muga Miyahara, PR Hiroaki Nakane; **middle:** Laforet advertising Fall 2003. **Page 83:** Laforet advertising Christmas 2001, AD/D Nagi Noda, D Keiichirou Oshima, PH Shoji Uchida, ST Shinichi Mita, H&MU Katsuya Kamo. **Page 84:** *CUTiE* (Takarajima Publishing) Hysteric Glamour advertorial December 9 1996, PH Takashi Homma, ST Sonya Park, H&MU Katsuya Kamo, M Miwako Ichikawa. **Page 86:** Hysteric Glamour advertising 1999. **Page 88 top row:** Hysteric Glamour advertising, 2002; **second row left:** PH Tamaki Kawaki; **second row center:** Hysteric Joey advertising 2006; **second row right:** Hysteric Glamour advertising 2004; **third row left:** 2001; **third row right:** 2005; **bottom row left:** 1995; **bottom row right:** Hysteric Glamour advertising 2003. **Page 89:** *CUTiE* (Takarajima Publishing) Hysteric Glamour advertorial December 1996, PH Rowland Kirishima, ST Sonya Park, H Kenjiro Akama, MU Naomi Kubota, M Miwako Ichikawa. **Page 90:** advertising 1999, PH Terry Richardson, ST Sabina Schraeder. **Page 91 top left:** "Cross Section" Patti Smith (Hysteric Glamour 2004); **top right:** *Daido Hysteric No. 6,* Daido Moriyama (Hysteric Glamour 1994); **bottom:** *Terry Richardson Hysteric Glamour* Terry Richardson (Hysteric Glamour 1998). **Page 92, 96 top:** *CUTiE* (Takarajima Publishing) June 24 1996 No. 83, PH Takashi Homma, ST Sonya Park, H Kenjiro Akama, MU Naomi Kubota, M Sayaka Yoshino. **Page 94 left:** *CUTiE* September 1 1995 No. 71, PH Rowland Kirishima, ST Sonya Park, H&MU Isao Tsuge, M Miwako Ichikawa, Maiko Yamada; **right:** *CUTiE* July 1 1995 No. 69, PH Rowland Kirishima, ST Sonya Park Park, H Kenjiro Akama, MU Naomi Kubota, M Miwako Ichikawa, Keith Martin. **Page 95:** *CUTiE* January 1995 No. 63, PH Takashi Homma, ST Sonya Park, H Kenjiro Akama, MU Hirokazu Niwa, M Miwako Ichikawa. **Page 97:** *CUTiE* Hysteric Glamour advertorial advertising May 12 1997 No.104, PH Takashi Homma ST Sonya Park, H&MU Katsuya Kamo, M Miwako Ichikawa. **Page 98:** *Popeye* (Magazine House, Ltd.) December 1977 No. 21, PH Hiroshi Yoda. **Page 99 top:** *Olive* (Magazine House, Ltd.) March 1985; **top right:** *Olive* (Magazine House, Ltd.) December 1984 No. 58, ST Mariko

Chikada, M Meg, Chris; **middle right:** *Popeye* (Magazine House, Ltd.) July 1994; **bottom right:** October 2002 No. 642, PH Katsumi Omori. **Pages 100–101:** *Libération Style 10* (Libération) Supplement to Libération No. 6971 October 11, 2003, PH Hiromix, H&MU Katsuya Kamo, M Ayumi (100 top), Tanabe (100 bottom) Kae, Sachi (101). **Page 102:** *Shinbiyo* (Shinbiyo Shuppan Co., Ltd) February 2005, PH Kazuo Arihara, H&MU Katsuya Kamo, M (top) Sachi, (bottom) Anna Kanehara; **middle left:** Notebooks courtesy of Katsuya Kamo A/W 97-98 Junya Watanabe Comme des Garçons; **middle right:** A/W 98-99 Junya Watanabe Comme des Garçons; **bottom left:** S/S 00 Junya Watanabe Comme des Garçons; **bottom right:** S/S 98 Junya Watanabe Comme des Garçons. **Page 103:** *Purple Fashion* (Olivier Zahm) F/W 2006/2007 No. 6, PH Hiromix, H&MU Katsuya Kamo. **Page 104:** *FRUiTS* (Lens Co., Ltd.) 1997 Super Lovers advertorial. **Page 105 top right:** Super Lovers advertising 2000; **bottom left:** Lover's Rock advertising. **Page 110:** *FRUiTS* (Lens Co., Ltd.) January 1999 No.18. **Page 112 top left spread:** June 1998 No.11; **middle left:** January 1999 No.18.; **middle right spread:** October 1997 No.3; **bottom spread:** February 2000 No.31. **Page 113:** top left: August 2003 No.73; **top middle:** May 2005 No. 94; **top right:** February 2000 No. 31; **middle right spread:** April 2004 No. 81; **bottom spread:** November 2006 No. 112. **Page 114 top left:** *TUNE* (Lens Co., Ltd.) July 2006 No. 21; **top middle spread:** May 2005 No. 6; **second row left:** July 2004 No. 2; **second row middle spread:** March 2005 No. 7; **bottom row left spread:** October 2005 No. 12; **right:** March 2005 No. 6. **Page 115 top left:** July 2004 No. 2; **top middle spread:** January 2006 No. 15; **second row left:** spread July 2006 No. 21; **second row right:** January 2006 No. 15; **bottom row left:** January 2006 No. 15; **bottom right:** July 2004 No. 2. **Page 119:** Artwork courtesy Masahiro Nakagawa. **Page 120 top:** PH Satoshi Saikusa, ST Mika Mizutani; **middle:** PH Jean-Baptiste Mondino, H&MU Topolino. **Page 121:** PH Satoshi Saikusa, ST Mika Mizutani. **Page 124:** *i-D* "The Conservative Issue" June 1986 No. 37, PH Mark Lebon. **Page 125 middle:** Artwork Christopher Nemeth; **bottom left:** PH Akira Gomi, ST Takayuki Katakura; **right:** PH Mike Owen, M Christopher Nemeth. **Page 126–129:** *Tokyo Hair* Masayuki Yoshinaga (Media Factory Co., Ltd 1999). **Page 138 top:** *Gothic & Lolita Bible* (Index Communications Co. Ltd.) November 2006 Vol. 23; **bottom:** *KERA* (Index Communications Co. Ltd.) January 2007 Vol. 102. **Page 139:** *KERA Maniax* (Index Communications Co. Ltd.) December 2006 Vol. 23. **Page 140 top left:** *KERA Maniax* February 2004 Vol. 2; **top right:** *Gothic & Lolita Bible* May 2007 Vol. 25; **bottom left:** *KERA* October 2006 Vol. 99; **bottom middle:** February 2001 Vol. 53; **bottom right:** October 2001 Vol. 61. **Page 141 top left:** *KERA Maniax* September 2006 Vol. 7; **top middle:** *Gothic & Lolita Bible* August 2006 Vol. 22; **top right:** *KERA Maniax* August 2005 Vol. 5; **second row left:** *Gothic & Lolita Bible* June 2003 Vol. 9; **second right:** *Gothic & Lolita Bible* November 2002 Vol. 7; **third row left:** *Gothic & Lolita Bible* December 2003 Vol. 11; **third row right:** *KERA Maniax* September 2003 Vol. 1; bottom: *KERA* April 1998 Vol. 1. **Page 143 bottom:** *Shimotsuma monogatari* (*Kamikaze Girls*) (TBS 2004). **Page 146 top and middle:** PH Takahiro Sakuma, H&MU Ko Aoki; **bottom:** PH Muga Miyahara, H&MU Noboru Tomizawa. **Page 147 top:** PH Muga Miyahara, H&MU Noboru Tomizawa; **bottom:** PH Takahiro Sakuma, H&MU Ko Aoki. **Page 148 top:** PH Makoto Ueda, M Trashlight Vision; **bottom:** PH Yousuke Komatsu, M 12012. **Page 149 top:** PH Susumu Miyawaki, M Antique Café; **bottom:** PH courtesy SEX POT ReVeNGe, M Megu. **Page 150-157:** PH Kai Regan. **Page 158:** *Livre Rosé Blanche: Cathedrale de la rose* (Midi Nette Co., Ltd) M Mana. **Page 160:** Moi-même-Moitié visuals courtesy Midi Nette Co.,Ltd. **Page 161 top row:** Moi dix mois "Beyond the Gate" 2006 tour pamphlet, AD Mana, D Centrino Duos, PH Kenji Tsukagoshi; **middle and bottom row:** *Livre Rosé Blanche: Cathedrale de la rose.* **Page 170:** *HUGE* (KODANSHA) February 2004 No. 4, PH JFK, Artwork by Shawn Stussy, M Hiroshi Fujiwara. **Pages 172–177:** PH Yasuhiro Hamazaki. **Page 178:** *NYLON guys* (NYLON HOLDING INC.) Summer 2007 PH Marvin Scott Jarrett M Nigo. **Page 183 top:** © 1976, 2007 SANRIO CO., LTD. APPROVAL NO. S8072327 **Page 184:** *Cherie* Cherie (Nowhere, 2002), *Beef or Chicken* Teriyaki Boys (Def Jam Recordings/APE SOUNDS, 2005). **Pages 186:** Graphics from *SIM* magazine, *HUGE* magazine poster, T-shirt graphic for the brand Teenagewolf. **Pages 187:** CD sleeve graphics for the band KZA, flyer graphics for club events Electro Discharge and Floor Clean, T-shirt graphic for the brand TILT. **Page 188:** Brand logo FAQQ, commissioned graphic for the brand P.A.M., graphic for the band 23 SKIDOO. **Page 189:** CD sleeve graphic for rap group SDP, logo for Balaclava Toys, T-shirt graphics for the label Crook Gadget, T-shirt graphic for toy manufacturer M-Ichigo and brand Neighborhood collaboration. **Page 192 top:** *smart* (Takarajima Publishing) October 16 2000 No. 93, PH Kyoji Takahashi, ST Takashi Kumagai, H&MU Isao Tsuge, M Tadanobu Asano; **bottom:** *relax* (Magazine House, Ltd.) September 2000, Illustration KAWS. **Page 193 top left:** *mini* March 2006, PH Keisuke Nagase, ST mick, H&MU Mihoko Fujiwara, M Kaela Kimura; **middle and bottom left:** *smart* October 16 2000 No.149, PH Kenshu Shintsubo, ST Yohei Usami, H&MU Akino, M Jun, Remi, Takahiro Okazawa, Kensei, Luke, Julian; **middle right:** *relax* September 2001 Illustration Kate Gibbs. **Page 196 top:** PH P.M. Ken; **bottom left:** "Captain Tsubasa" Illustration © Yoichi Takahashi. **Page 197:** Artwork copyright © Julian Opie. **Pages 198–199** Artwork P.M. Ken. **Page 201 top right:** "Captain Tsubasa" Illustration © Yoichi Takahashi. **Page 200 top:** PH Hiroki Nakamura; **bottom:** PH Masakazu Kunitake. **Page 201:** PH Masakazu Kunitake. **Page 203 inset left:** *SAMPLING: GIRLS' SNAP FASHION MAGAZINE* (Bunkasha Mook) September 1998 No.1, PH Masayuki Yoshinaga. **Pages 204–211:** Courtesy UNDER COVER. **Page 210:** Suzy Menkes, "Undercover: Strange, 'but beautiful'". *International Herald Tribune*, May 31, 2006, Style & Design. Copyright 2006 *International Herald Tribune.* **Page 219:** Artwork NEXUSVII. **Page 221 inset:** Artwork FAFI. **Page 224 top:** *Choki Choki* (Naigai Publishing Co., Ltd), PH Eisuke Fukumochi, M Yasushi Goto, Keisuke Yamada, Naoya Morishita, Shunsuke Mizutani; **bottom:** PH Masaharu Arisaka, M Taichiro Tsuboi; **bottom:** February 2007, PH Hideo Takamatsu. **Page 225:** PH and Artwork by Spank!. **Pages 224–229:** PH Gallermic Tanaka.

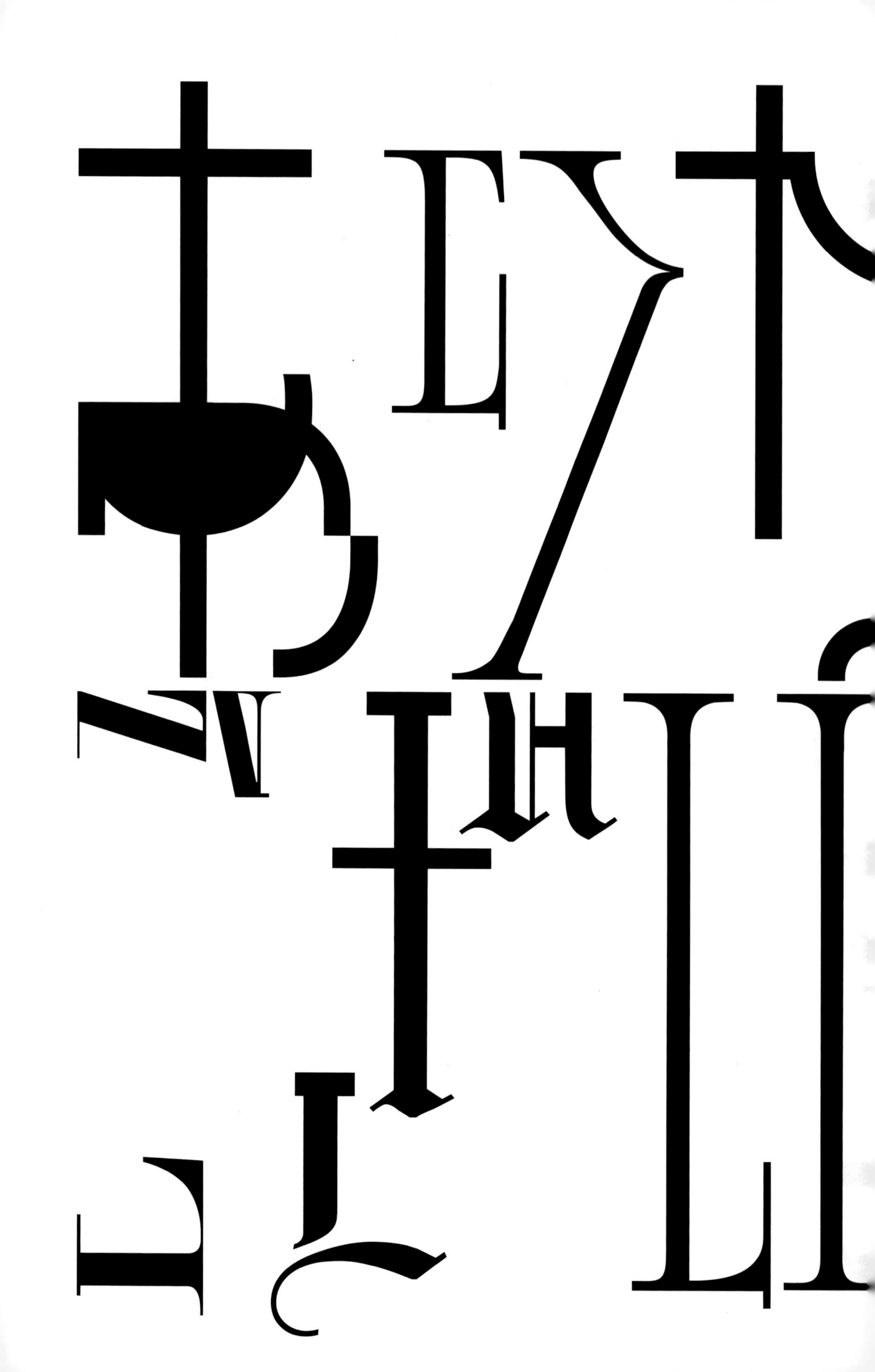

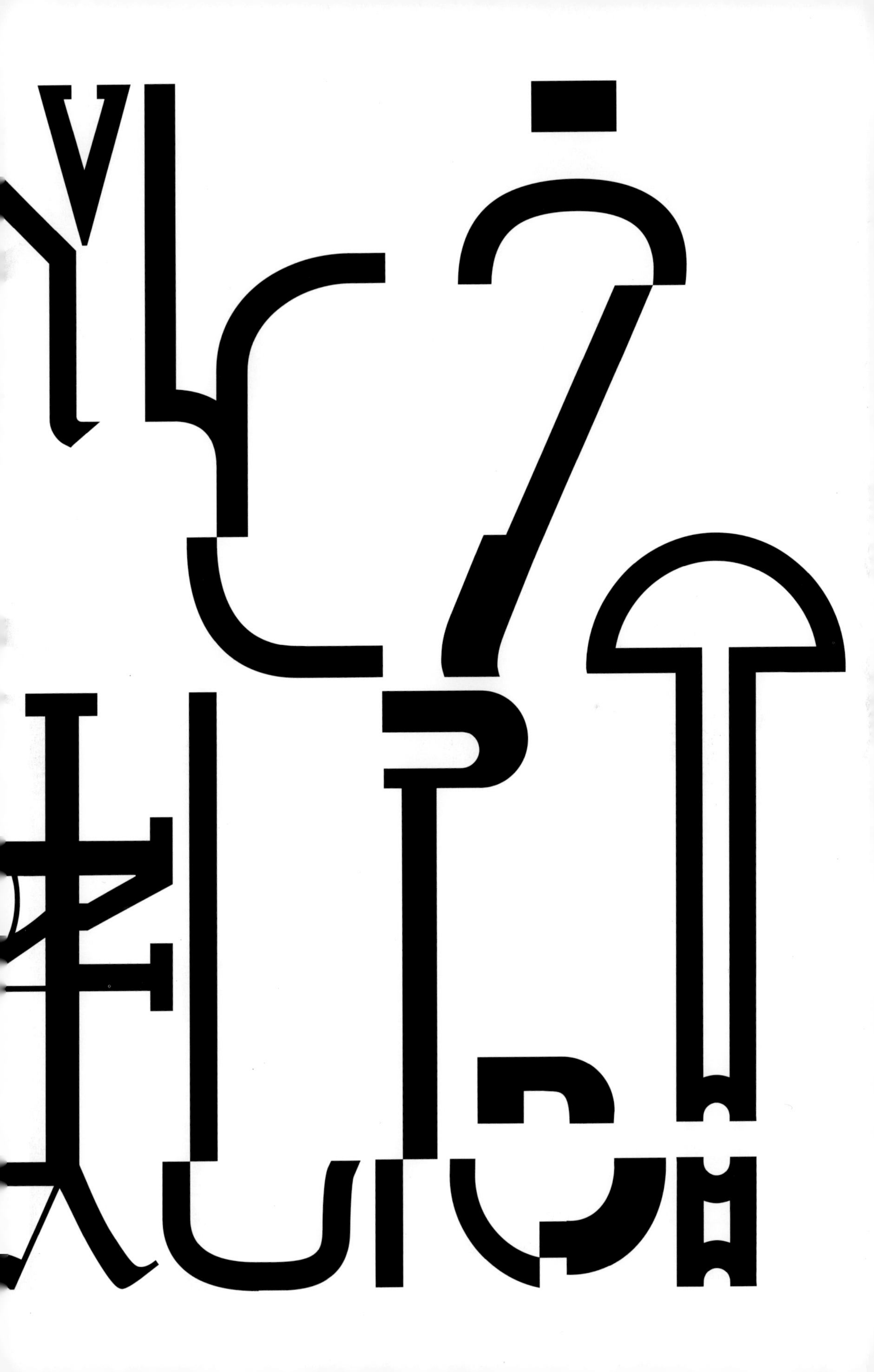

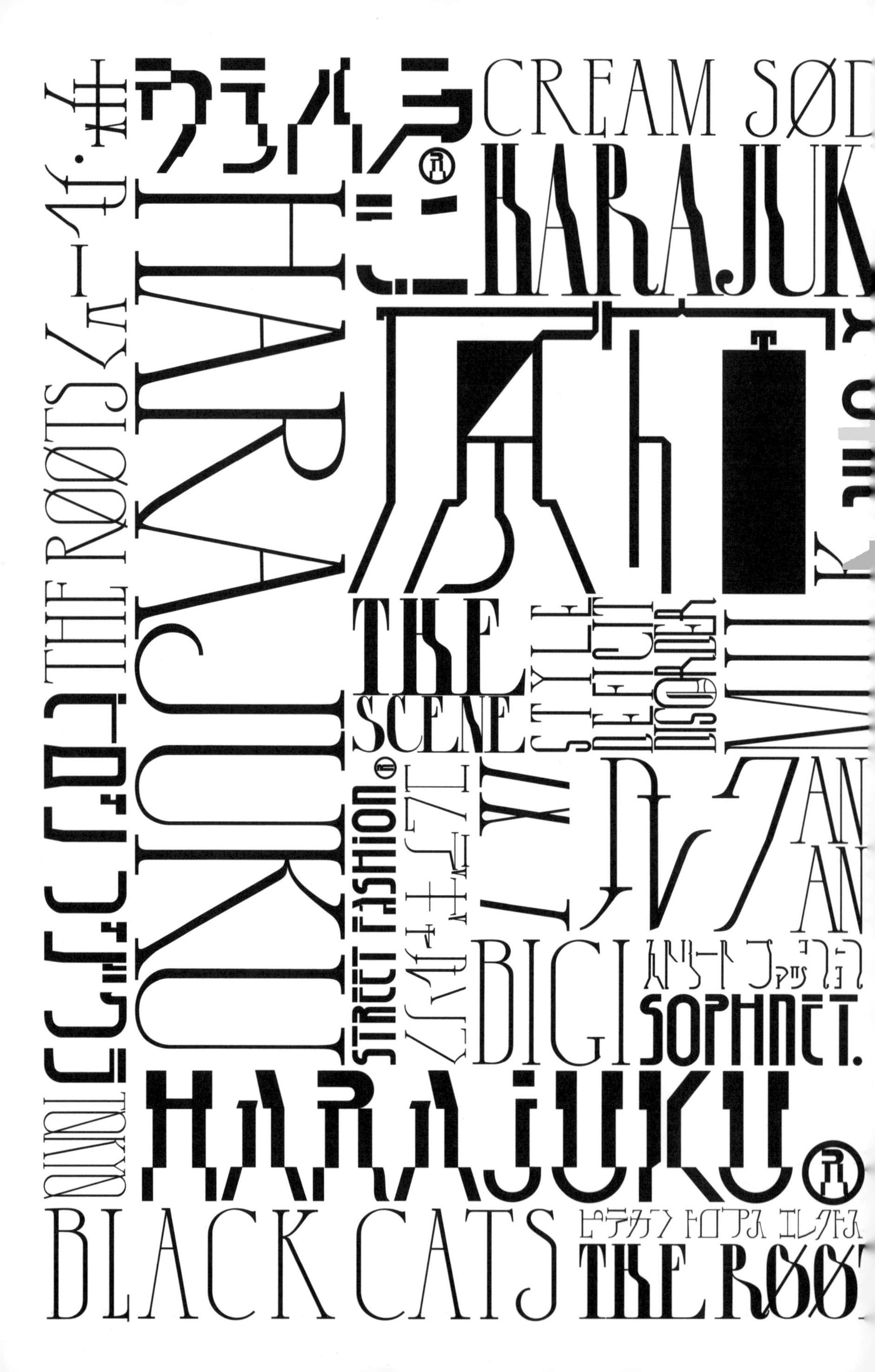
CREAM SØD
HARAJUK
HARAJUKU
THE RØØTS
THE SCENE
STREET FASHION
AN
AN
AN
BIGI
ストリートファッション
SOPHNET.
HARAJUKU
TOKYO
ピテカントロプス エレクトス
BLACK CATS
THE RØØT